Presented to

Natazhia

By

Leroy

On the Occasion of

a holiday

Date

18/ March 05

A MIND LIKE HIS

DISCOVERING THE MIND
OF JESUS THROUGH
PHILIPPIANS 4:8

Mike and Amy Nappa

BARBOUR
PUBLISHING, INC.
Uhrichsville, Ohio

A Mind Like His is another creative resource from the authors at Nappaland Communications, Inc. To contact the authors, access their web site at: www.Nappaland.com

Selections in this book marked with an asterisk (*) have been reprinted with permission from other sources. Please see the "Credits" section, which begins on page 267 of this book, for more detailed information regarding a reprinted selection's source.

Cover illustration © 2000 Susan Crawford.

Published by Barbour Publishing, Inc., P.O. Box 719, Uhrichsville, Ohio 44683 http://www.barbourbooks.com

Member of the
Evangelical Christian
Publishers Association

Printed in the United States of America.

DEDICATION

For Jim and Verna Olsen.
Thanks for bringing a bit more of Christ
into our everyday lives!

M&A

ABOUT THE COVER
ILLUSTRATION

Look closely on the cover of this book, and you'll find the key words of Philippians 4:8 hidden throughout the window illustration. The picture is the work of artist and calligrapher Susan Crawford, of Minerva, Ohio, who also illustrated the cover of Mike and Amy Nappa's book *A Heart Like His.*

Contents

Think about such things!

INTRODUCTION:
CAN YOU READ MY MIND?

Ever wish you could read minds—or been afraid someone else could read yours? I imagine sometimes what it would be like if our thoughts appeared above our heads in "thought balloons" like they do in the Sunday comics. For instance, if you were to read my mind that way today, the thought balloons above me might look something like this:

"I sure hope I can meet all my deadlines this week!"

"I wonder if whatever it is that made Amy sick last night is catching. . ."

"Maybe there'll be something good in today's mail."

"I'm going to hang that dog by his toenails if he doesn't quit barking!"

I could go on, but I'm sure you get the idea. My head is often filled with mundane worries and hopes, and too often absent of the things of God. Which makes me wonder, if we could "read" the mind of Jesus in little thought balloons, what we would find? Although I can't be 100 percent sure, my guess is that a glimpse into His mind would reveal exactly what the apostle Paul wrote about in Philippians 4:8 (NIV):

"Finally, brothers, whatever is true, whatever

is noble, whatever is right, whatever is pure, whatever is lovely, whatever is admirable—if anything is excellent or praiseworthy—think about such things."

And so I ask myself, "What lovely things are on Jesus' mind today? What truths? What admirable ideas are rolling around in His infinite intellect? And how can I train my thoughts to match His?"

That challenge is the one my wife (and frequent writing partner), Amy, and I attempted to answer with the book you now hold in your hands. For several months we immersed ourselves in the text of Philippians 4:8, and being writers, put the results of our little exploration down on paper. By no means do we think we've arrived at all the right answers—or are even asking all the right questions! But our prayer is that through this book, all of us (you included!) will at least begin a journey that will not end until that day in heaven when we truly have A Mind Like His.

So what do you think? Care to join us on this little trip into Philippians 4:8 and beyond? If so, turn the page and let's get started. After all, it's a journey not meant to be taken alone.

—MIKE NAPPA, 2000

1

Whatever Is

*T*rue

TRUE: (adjective) (1) being in accordance with the actual state of affairs; (2) steadfast and loyal. Synonyms: Genuine, honest, real, authentic, faithful.

A FISH STORY

A bank president was once in the need of a new teller to handle the cash window at his bank, so he wrote the following advertisement and placed it in the paper:

WANTED:
One bank teller trainee. No experience necessary, but honesty is a must. Bring references.

The following day a line of men and women wishing to apply for the job circled around the bank and into the parking lot outside. The bank president walked down the line looking over the applicants. "How do I know you won't steal my customers' money when my back is turned?" the president gruffly asked a neat-looking man near the front of the line.

Gesturing to the woman next to him, the man replied, "Why, my mother can vouch for my honesty, sir!"

"Not good enough," grumbled the banker. Next he stopped by an attractive couple midway through the line. "How do I know you won't steal my customers' money when my back is turned?" he asked the woman.

"Why, my fiancé will vouch for me, sir!" the woman responded, pointing to the man with her in line.

"Not good enough," the old banker said again. Then his eyes fell on two fishing buddies near the end of the line. He strode to the younger of the two and asked, "How do I know you won't steal my customers' money when my back is turned?"

The young man smiled and gestured to his buddy, "Because I'm always truthful, sir, and I promise I won't steal from you." The banker snorted and started to turn away, but the young man stopped him and said, "Wait! My fishing partner will vouch for the truth of my words, sir!"

The older fisherman nodded and stepped forward. "It's true, sir," he said. "You can trust my friend, and I'll tell you why. Last Thursday I was ill and he went out to fish all by himself. When he got back, he told me he'd been fishing all day and hadn't gotten a single bite!"

The bank president smiled, and the young fisherman got the job!

The Truth about Lying

A psychology study at the University of Virginia in Charlottesville recently asked seventy-seven volunteers to record the number of lies they told in a week. Seven volunteers reported never lying once; the other seventy people confessed to lying

1535 times during that seven-day period.

In a 1998 survey of twenty thousand middle school and high school students, 92 percent admitted that they'd lied to their parents in the previous year. Nearly three out of four of these students (73 percent) also said they were "serial liars"—meaning they told lies on a weekly basis.

Roughly seven of every ten Americans (72 percent) agree with the statement "There is no such thing as absolute truth"—even though belief in that statement is inherently contradictory (i.e., if there is no absolute truth, then that statement also cannot be absolutely true, meaning absolute truth must therefore exist).

Nearly half of "evangelicals" (42 percent) and nearly two-thirds of "born-again Christians" (62 percent) also agree with the statement that "there is no such thing as absolute truth."

Although 90 percent of college students say cheating is "always wrong," roughly one-third of those same students (32 percent) report having cheated on classwork in the past year.

About three-quarters of college students (74 percent) believe that "most people will cheat or lie when it is necessary to get what they want."

Nearly one-third of high school and college students report that they are willing to lie in a resume, job application, or interview to get what they want. Additionally, two out of five college students (39 percent) admit having lied to a boss while on a job. Just over one out of three (35 percent) admits to having lied to a customer within the past year.

Ninety-one percent of Americans as a whole lie regularly.

One out of every five Americans tells a conscious, premeditated lie each day.

Men lie more than women.

Two-thirds of Americans believe there's nothing wrong with telling a lie.

Those we love are also those we lie to the most. Consider: 86 percent of Americans confess lying to their parents; 75 percent say they've lied to friends; 73 percent admit lying to a sibling, and that same number also admit lying to a lover; and 69 percent say they've lied to a spouse.

❧

LIAR, LIAR*

by Leslie L. Nunn

It's eight years old. It's been great. But it's starting to fall apart. First it was the brake pads. Then the oil gasket. Now it's a slipping transmission. Maybe I should trade it in and get something shiny and new before I have to have one more thing fixed. If I'm lucky, the guy who does the trade-in inspection at the dealership won't drive the car and experience the delayed shifting from first to second. Or maybe the car will cooperate until I unload it. I don't need to tell him about the problem. I mean, it's his job to do the inspection, right? Besides, car dealers don't have the best reputation for being up-front and honest. So what would it hurt to just keep quiet?

An informal poll revealed that car salesmen make the list as one of the most dishonest elements of American culture, along with these others who hold powerful positions in society: police, politicians, government officials, and lawyers. Newspaper reports are replete with accounts of individuals who fail to stand by their word. Perhaps their examples are defining society's expectations of truth and reinforcing Sir Walter Scott's famous line, "Oh what a tangled web we weave when first we practice to deceive." Yet colleges and universities across the United States offer courses in business ethics and ethical theory. One school, Wheaton College, even includes a unit on lying in its ethics class. They are studying the questions: Is it right? Is it moral? Is it true? . . .

Ancient philosophers and ethicists believed there were four times when it was ethical to lie:

    (1) To save a life
    (2) To save a friendship
    (3) To mislead an enemy
    (4) To maintain peace in the home

And today? According to business ethicist J. Gregory Dees, Ph.D., many people will make their truthfulness conditional on what they expect of a particular circumstance or situation. In the setting of negotiating with a car dealer, most people lie.

"They expect others to lie to them, so they do, too," he says. "Lying here doesn't make it right on an ethical scale, but in their minds, it seems fair. They might find it distasteful and are uncomfortable, but they do it because they have to play the game."

Dees doesn't believe this is a good thing, even from an economic bargaining point of view, because it's inequitable and gets people to behave in ways that in other settings are improper. His goal is not simply to present a moral argument about why it's okay or not to lie. He hopes to offer a practical solution of how to help people create trust in settings so that lying isn't considered necessary.

Dr. Alan Strudler, a professor at the Wharton School at the University of Pennsylvania, opposes Dees. He believes there's nothing wrong with this kind of deception in negotiation. It's healthy. It's a way for people in difficult circumstances to signal the truth in some roundabout way. It's only the naïve people who are hurt. If a car dealer is simply misleading someone about the price he'll accept, that's okay.

"I believe this approach is wrong and dangerous," says Dees. "It makes it too easy for people to excuse behavior. Honesty doesn't necessarily require candor, but it does require that you don't lie." For example, if someone is negotiating to buy a house, it's understood in our culture that he won't disclose to the seller the highest price he is willing to pay.

Cultural norms change and vary from society to society. Americans used to haggle on prices in grocery stores, but not anymore. Should this kind of deception remain the norm? If not, how should we change it?

"We can preach honesty," Dees says, "but people won't change their behavior just because someone says it's the right thing to do. If they feel vulnerable, they will behave in a way they don't like but that they feel is necessary."

Saturn car manufacturers have tested possible solutions. Car prices are posted; there is no negotiating. All buyers get the same deal. The sales people are there to help customers and are compensated differently than in a traditional dealership. Studies have shown that Saturn customers have a high degree of satisfaction with the car purchase program and a trust in Saturn products. There apparently are ways to set up systems to reduce the incentive for dishonesty.

No doubt such practices of promoting truth would be honoring to God. When He handed down the Law through Moses to His people in the wilderness, God commanded them, "You shall not give false testimony against your neighbor." Though truth is a concept for which the Old Testament has no distinct word, it generally is used to mean "constant, permanent, faithful, reliable." The word itself appears 227 times in the NIV translation of the Bible. Throughout the New Testament, Jesus teaches His disciples and says, "I tell you the truth. . . ." He is "the way, the truth, and the life."

"The biblical information is so overwhelmingly supportive of truthfulness," says Dr. David B. Fletcher, associate professor of philosophy at Wheaton College. "Lying represents something diametrically opposed to the God of truth, and most people, when surveyed, claim it's important to be truthful. They recoil at the suggestion that they lie. But I'm not sure Christians are as exemplary in their actions as they should be. We often assume we are the truthful ones; I don't know that there's any evidence to support that. Christians seem about as honest as the next person, not any more so."

The biblical example of truth contradicts a popular definition that might be summed up in these comments posted on an Internet Truth and Ethics message board: "You are your own truth. You must decide what is true and false to you. You must mold and create your own reality. You must find the truth that suits you and know that no one's truth is the same as your own."

In one of the most riveting events before Jesus' crucifixion, He stands before Pilate and says that He has come into the world to testify to the truth. "What is truth?" Pilate asks. Author and minister Frederick Buechner suggests that, contrary to the traditional view that his question is cynical, "It is possible that he asks it with a lump in his throat. Instead of Truth, Pilate has only expedience. His decision to throw Jesus to the wolves is expedient. Pilate views man as alone in the universe with nothing but his own courage and ingenuity to see him through. It is enough to choke up anybody.

"Pilate asks, 'What is truth?' and for years there have been politicians, scientists, theologians, philosophers, poets, and so on to tell him. The sound they make is like the sound of empty pails falling down the cellar stairs. Jesus doesn't answer Pilate's question. He just stands there."

God has given us the truth in the person of Jesus. We should always keep our lives measured by His standards. To be blameless. To expose ourselves before God. Adam and Eve disobeyed God in the garden and didn't tell the truth. Of course, God knew of their disobedience, and it grieved Him. When we don't walk in the truth, we sin before God and others. But when we come into agreement with God about our wrong actions through confession, He forgives us.

One of the lines in a favorite prayer of confession says, "We confess that we have sinned against You in thought, word, and deed; By what we have done, and by what we have left undone." The sin of omission (not telling the truth) is just as grievous to God as telling an outright lie.

It means that failing to inform the dealer of a problem with the car during a trade-in is deception. What good is gained by being dishonest with others or with God? How can we be transformed into His image if we cover those things we don't want Him to know about? If we surrender to Him and seek to know and speak the truth in all things, we will be changed. In the process, we will change our culture and our world.

FACE THE MUSIC*

by Amy Nappa and Jody Brolsma

"I was a typical snoopy little sister," admits Jody. "Since I was at home when my brother and sisters were at school, I managed to explore their rooms and get into all kinds of trouble."

One afternoon, Jody slipped into Jill's room to check out the toys that would eventually be hers (as the fourth of five children, Jody already knew what hand-me-downs were). Jill's Raggedy Ann doll was lying on the bed. "To this day, I'm not sure what prompted me to do what came next," says Jody. At any rate, she found her brother's fake vampire blood (another "no-no") and used it to "draw" all over poor Raggedy Ann's face. "I remember holding the 'bleeding' doll, thinking, *Someone's going to see this. I'd better hide it.*" So Jody turned the doll face down on the pillow and left the scene of the crime.

Our dad was also the victim of Jody's afternoon explorations. We all knew that he kept a pack of Wrigley's Doublemint Gum in his desk drawer. Chalk it up to budding creativity, but Jody opened the package, licked off the sugary coating, and made a row of teeth marks on each stick of gum. Then she neatly rewrapped each stick and placed the package back in the drawer, certain that no one would find out.

Well, as the saying goes, the truth will find you out. Jill came home and turned over her doll to find a gory mess. (Plus, Joel discovered that his fake vampire blood was missing, and Mom wasn't too happy to find that one of her nice pillowcases was ruined.) Dad came home to enjoy a stick of gum and discovered a preschool art project instead. In both cases, the truth couldn't be hidden very long. It eventually came to light and consequences were felt by many family members.

The truth will always come to light. Max Lucado writes, "The ripple of today's lie is tomorrow's wave and next year's flood." Our dishonesty, whether it is discovered today or far into the future, has impact on our lives and on the lives of those we love. Hearts are stained with mistrust. Confidence is marred.

There's a story about a man who conned his way into the orchestra of the emperor of China. Though the man had no musical talent, he faked his way through each practice, simply holding the flute in place and moving his fingers while the other musicians played. Because of his deception, he was paid well and lived comfortably.

Then the emperor requested a solo from each musician. The flutist panicked and pretended to be sick. Unfortunately, the royal physician wasn't fooled. When the day came for the flutist to play his solo, he took poison and killed himself. This incident led to a phrase that we've all used: "He refused to face the music."

The Bible speaks repeatedly of men and women who tried to hide the truth. Adam and Eve. Cain. Achan. David. Haman. (And that's just the Old Testament!) Their deceit was uncovered and the effects were felt generations after them.

When you're tempted to be dishonest, have the courage to face the music. No lie ever glorified God. And no lie has ever remained in the dark for long.

IF I TELL. . .

if i tell
you may go.
if i am silent
you'll never know.
honesty may bring loss,
but without it love cannot grow.

SPEAKING OF TRUTH. . .

If you tell the truth,
you don't have to remember anything.
MARK TWAIN,
as recorded in Quoteland.com

"Truth, like Jesus Christ, may always be denied, persecuted, combated, wounded, martyred, crucified; but it always lives again and rises again and cannot be wrenched out of the human heart."

POPE JOHN PAUL II,
in *Fear Not*

"Do you not profess to have, and hold, and therefore teach the truth? I profess only to have caught glimpses of her white garments—those, I mean, of which the abstract truth of which you speak. But I have seen that which is eternally beyond her: the ideal in the real, the living truth, not the truth that I can think, but the truth that thinks itself, that thinks me, that God has thought, yea, that God is, the truth being true to itself and to God and to man—Christ Jesus, my Lord, who knows, and feels, and does the truth. I have seen Him, and I am both content and unsatisfied. For in Him are hid all the treasures of wisdom and knowledge."

GEORGE MACDONALD, in
Annals of a Quiet Neighborhood

"The truth is incontrovertible. Panic may resent it, ignorance may deride it, malice may distort it, but there it is."

WINSTON CHURCHILL, in a 1916 address to
England's House of Commons

"I don't want any yes-men around me. I want everybody to tell me the truth even if it costs them their jobs."

Movie mogul SAMUEL GOLDWYN,
as quoted by Adam Christing in
Comedy Comes Clean 2

"The greatest trick the devil ever pulled was convincing the world he didn't exist."
VERBAL KENT
(as portrayed by Kevin Spacey)
in *The Usual Suspects*

"To walk in the truth is more than to give assent to it. It means to apply it to one's behavior. He who 'walks in the truth' is an integrated Christian in whom there is no dichotomy between profession and practice. On the contrary, there is in him an exact correspondence between his creed and his conduct. Such conformity of life to the truth on the part of his children brought [the apostle] John greater joy than anything else. To him truth mattered."

JOHN R.W. STOTT
in *The Epistles of John*

"Live truth instead of professing it."
ELBERT HUBBARD,
as quoted in *The Book of Wisdom*

"Truth is always about something, but reality is that about which truth is."

C. S. LEWIS, in *God in the Dock*

"I hope people will say [of me], 'You know, Jimmy Carter made a lot of mistakes, but he never told me a lie.'"

Former president JIMMY CARTER,
in a 1976 interview with Bill Moyers

❦

The Word on Truth...

"If you abide in My word, then you are truly disciples of Mine; and you shall know the truth, and the truth shall make you free."

JOHN 8:31–32 NASB

Jesus said to him, "I am the way, the truth, and the life. No one comes to the Father except through Me."

JOHN 14:6 NKJV

All your words are true [Lord];
all your righteous laws are eternal.
PSALM 119:160 NIV

Speak the truth so that you cannot be criticized. Then those who are against you will be ashamed because there is nothing bad to say about us.

TITUS 2:8 NCV

Our responsibility is never to oppose the truth, but to stand for the truth at all times.

2 CORINTHIANS 13:8 NLT

Truth Aflame

"I must know the truth," the man said earnestly. Thomas Hauker gazed into his friend's eyes and saw the hunger, the desperate need behind those words. It was ironic, really. After all, Thomas should've been asking for favors from his friend, and not vice versa, as was the case that terrible day in 1555.

You see, Thomas Hauker had been condemned to die the very next morning. Sentenced to be burned at the stake for his dogged refusal to renounce his Christian faith. Tomorrow he would be led to the top of a mountain of wood, bound to a stake at its center, then callously lit on fire to burn in agony until he was dead, dead, dead.

Yet at the end, Thomas asked for no favors. And he found himself facing a friend who spoke with grave urgency.

"Thomas," the friend whispered, "I have to ask you this favor. I need to know if what the others say about the grace of God is true. Tomorrow, when they burn you at the stake, if the pain is tolerable and your mind is still at peace, lift your hands above your head. Do it right before you die." The friend looked sorrowfully into Thomas's face, paused a moment, then spoke one last time. "Thomas," he said, "I have to know."

Thomas Hauker spoke gently, reassuring his friend and promising to reveal whether or not God's grace was still true even in the worst of life's circumstances, even while burning at that stake.

Next morning, the martyr was led to his fiery destination. The flames were kindled, then raged, ravaging the man who refused to bow to any but Christ. In the heat of it all, Thomas Hauker's body sagged, slowly being consumed by the merciless heat. At last, his skin was burnt to a crisp, his fingers were gone, and most in the crowd assumed the man was finally dead.

But those who turned away then missed the most miraculous sight. Suddenly the "dead" man stirred. In silence, he raised his still-burning hands high over what was left of his head. He clapped those hands together. Once. Twice. Three times. Then, at last, his arms fell to his sides and he moved no more.

The crowd was silent at first, and then moments later joined Thomas Hauker in thunderous applause and praise for God. For just before he died, the martyr had testified one last time to the truth—no, to the Truth, of God. And that made all the difference.

On September 2, 1993, Charles Colson delivered the Templeton Address at the University of Chicago, and in that speech exposed four great myths that have masked the truth in American society for decades. He called them. . .

THE FOUR HORSEMEN*

by Charles Colson

Four great myths define our times—the four horsemen of the present apocalypse.

The first myth is the goodness of man. The first horseman rails against heaven with the presumptuous question: Why do bad things happen to good people? He multiplies evil by denying its existence.

This myth deludes people into thinking that they are always the victims, never villains; always deprived, never depraved. It dismisses responsibility as the teaching of a darker age. It can excuse any crime, because it can always blame something else—a sickness of society or a sickness of the mind.

One writer called the modern age "the golden age of exoneration." When guilt is dismissed as the illusion of narrow minds, then no one is accountable, even to his conscience.

The irony is that this should come alive in this century, of all centuries, with its gulags and death camps and killing fields. As G. K. Chesterton once said, the doctrine of original sin is the only philosophy empirically validated by the centuries of recorded human history.

It was a holocaust survivor who exposed this myth most eloquently. Yehiel Dinur was a witness during the trial of Adolf Eichmann. Dinur entered the courtroom and stared at the man behind the bulletproof glass—the man who had presided over the slaughter of millions. The court was hushed as a victim confronted a butcher.

Then suddenly Dinur began to sob, and collapsed to the floor. Not out of anger or bitterness. As he explained later in an interview, what struck him at that instant was a terrifying realization. "I was afraid about myself," Dinur said. "I saw that I am capable to do this. . .exactly like he."

The reporter interviewing Dinur understood precisely. "How was it possible for a man to act as Eichmann acted?" he asked. "Was he a monster? A madman? Or was he perhaps something even more terrifying. . . .Was he normal?"

Yehiel Dinur, in a moment of chilling clarity, saw the skull beneath the skin. "Eichmann," he concluded, "is in all of us."

Jesus said it plainly: "That which proceeds out of the man, that is what defiles the man" (Mark 7:20 NASB).

The second myth of modernity is the promise of coming utopia. The second horseman arrives with sword and slaughter.

This is the myth that human nature can be perfected by government; that a new Jerusalem can be built using the tools of politics.

From the birth of this century, ruthless ideologies claimed history as their own. They moved from nation to nation on the strength of a promised utopia. They pledged to move the world, but could only stain it with blood.

In communism and fascism we have seen rulers who bear the mark of Cain as a badge of honor; who pursue a savage virtue, devoid of humility and humanity. We have seen more people killed in this century by their own governments than in all its wars combined. We have seen every utopian experiment fall exhausted from the pace of its own brutality.

Yet utopian temptations persist, even in the world's democracies—stripped of their terrors perhaps, but not of their risks. The political illusion still deceives, whether it is called the great society, the new covenant, or the new world order. In each case it promises government solutions to our deepest needs for security, peace, and meaning.

The third myth is the relativity of moral values. The third horseman sows chaos and confusion.

This myth hides the dividing line between good and evil, noble and base. It has thus created a crisis in the realm of truth. When a society abandons its transcendent values, each individual's moral vision becomes purely personal and finally equal. Society becomes the sum total of individual preferences, and since no preference is morally preferable, anything that can be dared will be permitted.

This leaves the moral consensus for our laws and manners in tatters. Moral neutrality slips into moral relativism. Tolerance substitutes for truth, indifference for religious conviction. And in the end, confusion undercuts all our creeds.

The fourth modern myth is radical individualism. The fourth horseman brings excess and isolation.

This myth dismisses the importance of family, church, and community; denies the value of sacrifice; and elevates individual rights and pleasures as the ultimate social value.

But with no higher principles to live by, men and women suffocate under their own expanding pleasures. Consumerism becomes empty and leveling, leaving society full of possessions but drained of ideals. This is what Vaclav Havel calls "totalitarian consumerism."

A psychologist tells the story of a despairing young woman, spent in an endless round of parties, exhausted by the pursuit of pleasure. When told she should simply stop, she responded, "You mean I don't have to do what I want to do?"

As author George MacDonald once wrote, "The one principle of hell is 'I am my own.'"

I have seen firsthand the kind of society these deadly myths create. In seventeen years, I have been in more prisons that I can count, in more nations than I can name. I have seen the face of the crisis of modernity in real human faces.

The myth of human goodness tells men and women they are not responsible for their action, that everyone is a victim. "Poverty is the cause of crime," said a U.S. attorney general three decades ago. "Looters are not to blame for looting," said a U.S. president. Thus excused, millions refused accountability for their behavior; crime soared—and is today the great plague on civilized societies.

Utopianism, however, assures us that crime can be solved by government policy. On the left, that means rehabilitation; on the right, more and more tough laws to scare people straight. But, our efforts prove futile. In the past thirty years, the prison population in America has increased five-fold. But violent crime has increased just as fast.

For criminals are not made by sociological or environmental or economic forces. They are created by their own moral choices. Institutions of cold steel and bars are unable to reach the human heart, and so they can neither deter nor rehabilitate.

A decade ago, social scientist James Q. Wilson searched for some correlation between crime and social forces. He discovered that in the late nineteenth century, when the nation was rapidly industrializing—conditions that should have caused more crime to increase—crime actually declined. The explanation? At the time a powerful spiritual awakening was sweeping across America, inspiring moral revival and social re-newal. By contrast, in the affluent 1920s when there should have been less economic incentive for lawlessness, crime increased. Why? In the wake of Freud and Darwin, religion fell from favor. In Wilson's words, "The educated classes began to repudiate moral uplift."

A similar study in England by Professor Christie Davies found that crime was lowest a century ago when three out of four young Britons were enrolled in Sunday school. Since then, Sunday school attendance has declined, and crime has correspondingly increased.

Crime is a mirror of community's moral state. A society cannot long survive if the demands of human dignity are not written on our hearts. No number of police can enforce order; no threat of punishment can create it. Crime and violence frustrate every political answer, because there can be no solution apart from character and creed.

But relativism and individualism have undermined the traditional beliefs that once informed our character and defined our creed. There are no standards to guide us. Dostoyevsky's diagnosis was correct: Without God, everything is permissible; crime is inevitable.

These myths constitute a threat for all of us, regardless of our culture or the faith communities we represent. The four horsemen of the present apocalypse lead away from the cloud and fire of God's presence into a barren wilderness. Modernity was judged by the heights of aspirations. Today it must be judged by the depth of its decadence. That decadence has marked the West most deeply; this makes it imperative that we understand the struggle for the soul of western civilization.

A Prayer of John Calvin

O Lord, heavenly Father, in whom is the fullness of light and wisdom, enlighten our minds by Your Holy Spirit, and give us grace to receive Your Word with reverence and humility, without which no one can understand Your truth. For Christ's sake.
Amen.

Renowned worship leader Dennis Jernigan knows firsthand what it's like to suffer under misperceptions about shame and guilt. For that reason he wrote the following essay, which we're honored to share with you here.

The Truth about
Shame and Guilt*

by Dennis Jernigan

Shame and guilt have been with us since the Fall. In the first days of the beautiful Garden of Eden, Adam and Eve knew no shame or guilt. They were naked yet had no covering because purity requires none (see Gen. 2:25). When sin entered their world, it brought guilt and shame, and they suddenly felt a need to cover themselves. That's what shame and guilt do to us. They make us want to head for cover and hide.

But shame and guilt aren't always bad. Whether they're used for good or evil depends on who's using them. God lovingly uses shame and guilt to correct His children. The Enemy uses the same things to condemn and attack our true identity. Our goal, as new creations, is to uncover the lies of the Enemy and to discover the truth of who our Father says we are. Understanding the roles of shame and guilt improves our ability to give and receive love—with Father God and with other people.

When we come face to face with our sin, we rightly feel ashamed. We feel disgrace and dishonor and unworthiness. But if we allow shame to do godly work, it will bring us to the foot of the Cross, the forgiveness of God will fill our hearts with hope, and the imparted righteousness of Jesus Christ will replace our cloak of shame. God never meant shame to stay in our hearts; it is only meant to bring us to Him. Shame, when left intact, brings a constant barrage against our self-worth and identity—a perpetual onslaught of the Enemy. Shame attacks our identity and tries to keep us down. If our identity is constantly attacked, how can we understand who we really are? Before I understood the healing power of Christ's love, I walked around clothed in feelings of unworthiness, and I thought often of how embarrassed I would be if anyone knew of my sin. I was ashamed.

Shame said to me: If I am found out, I will be rejected. The Enemy wants us to feel deliberate coldness or disregard. However, God's convicting truth tells us that God is opposed to the proud but gives grace to the humble. He is waiting for us to honestly accept responsibility for our sin.

Shame says: If I am found out, I will be abandoned. The Enemy wants us to feel forsaken and deserted. But God says He will not leave us or forsake us. We are the ones who leave and forsake Him.

Shame says: If I am found out, I will be condemned. The Enemy wants us to be disapproved of, to be judged and sentenced, to feel unfit for use. But God says there is no more condemnation for those who are in Christ Jesus (see Rom. 8:1).

Shame is a feeling. Guilt, on the other hand, is more than a feeling; it is also a fact. When I do something I know is wrong, I "feel" guilty; I feel the separation due to the conviction of the Holy Spirit. But there's more to it than just a feeling. When I sin, I am indeed guilty. Guilt is the fact that I am responsible for the commission of an offense. Guilt reminds us of who and whose we are and helps us keep our eyes focused on Jesus. Guilt can have a holy effect upon my heart. Like shame, guilt is good when it causes us to see our need for Jesus. But if we remain in our guilty state, we are left fugitives, fearing, What if we are found out? Past sins, when left unconfessed, are like weights if we do not cut them loose. They drag us deep into deception and self-pity, and the miry clay becomes hard and binding. Habitual sins, sins we still battle, are like chains around our feet, and they keep us from climbing into the higher places of God's heart.

Because of the shame I associated with my past sins, I used to shut myself off from others, thinking that living without love was better than possible rejection. Yet all I found in this state was death. To lock out everyone is a lot like the way I picture hell—no love given; no love received. But as I began to open my heart to God's love for me, I realized it was my guilt and shame that was behind my fear of rejection. Once I was able to deal with my guilt and shame at the Cross of Christ, I was able to open myself up to love others and to receive love from others—even though the possibility of rejection remained.

> When I was born again in Christ,
>   shame lost its power because my
>   nakedness was covered by Jesus.
> When I came to Christ,
>   guilt became a tool in the hand of the Holy
>   Spirit to purify my heart.
> When Jesus dealt with my sin,
>   shame had no more place in my life.
> I can now come boldly before the throne
>   of grace,
> because my sin-debt has been paid in full.

❧

Not long ago, Mike was fortunate enough to interview award-winning author Philip Yancey over lunch at a downtown Denver eatery. During their chat, the conversation turned to Christianity and why Yancey believed it to be true. Here's what Philip had to say. . .

PHILIP YANCEY ON
WHY CHRISTIANITY IS TRUE

Mike Nappa: Philip, the question we're often asked is this: How do you know that Christianity is true? Why are you a Christian and not some other religion or no religion at all?

Philip Yancey: Bishop William Temple in England said this phrase. The first time I heard it, it struck me as strange. I had to think about it a lot: "In God is no un-Christlikeness at all."

What that means, in common English, is if you want to know what God is like, look at Jesus. Look at Jesus. If you read just the Old Testament that we've talked about, you will see failure after failure after failure. Nobody's content. God's irritable, unhappy, disappointed. The Israelites are irritable, unhappy, disappointed, and almost wiped off the face of the earth. When the Old Testament ends, David's tromped on by Syria and Persia and Babylon, and the next few years, they're tromped on by Greece and by Rome. It's a disaster. And in the midst of all that, the prophets have said, "Yeah, but something's going to change. Something's going to change."

Now nobody predicted what actually did happen. None of the people of the time recognized it, and that's when God became a human being. . . . Now, we know that Jesus was not kind of God's last-second idea. He had it in mind from the foundation of the world, as the epistles tell us. But why did Jesus come? What difference does He make?

Well, if you're just stuck with the God Who is revealed in the Old Testament, compared to Jesus, you're missing a lot—missing an awful lot. And God in Jesus found a way to bridge the gap. He showed us what God is like—in God is no un-Christlikeness at all—and He showed us what we should be like. And so, the cross is an appropriate emblem because it's these two lines that come together and never again meet. That's what Jesus does, and Jesus really doesn't allow us the option of considering Him just one of many. He's pretty clear. "I am the One. I am the One sent by God to bring the world to God."

Nappa: In most of your books, you seem to work hard to challenge us believers to face the truth about a relationship with Jesus. Why do you suppose we need that kind of challenge?

Yancey: Well, the reason I emphasize that, I suppose, is that I was brought up in a church that told you not to think. And they would say, "Don't question. Just believe." And the things I was told to just believe I found out later were lies, a lot of them. "Just believe that black people are inferior to white people." And they'd point to a verse in Genesis that would tell the curse of Canaan and all that, and I, for a time, I threw out the whole [Christian] thing because I realized,

"Man, this is a bunch of nonsense."

Later I realized, "Well, yeah, that's true. It is a bunch of nonsense, but somewhere in there is a core of truth that is the most important thing in the world. What is that core of truth?" So my process ever since has been to "reclaim those words." They were spoiled, they were distorted, and often they were the opposite [of truth]. . . . So I think my process as the pilgrim is just to go back and reclaim those words and find truth that I could claim for myself, and then for anybody else who happened to follow along.

A PRAYER FOR TRUTH

*by Brooke Foss Westcott,
Bishop of Durham*

Almighty God, Who sent the Spirit of truth to us to guide us into all truth: so rule our lives by Your power that we may be truthful in thought and word and deed. May no fear or hope ever make us false in act or speech; cast out from us whatsoever loves or makes a lie, and bring us all into the perfect freedom of Your truth, through Jesus Christ our Lord.

2

Whatever Is

*N*oble

NOBLE: (adjective) (1) possessing outstanding qualities; (2) superiority of mind or character, or of ideals or morals. Synonyms: honorable, moral, lofty, virtuous, grand.

❧

WHEN HUCK FINN MET
A NOBLEMAN (OR TWO)

It is a classic moment in literary history, that day when Huckleberry Finn and the runaway slave, Jim, first came into contact with nobility.

Huck and Jim had taken off on a raft down the mighty Mississippi River, running to freedom (for Jim) and away from "sivilization" (for Huck). Along the way, the two runaways encountered two comrades in flight. When the two new travelers joined up with Huck and Jim, the boy and the slave were let in on a noble secret.

"Ah, you would not believe me," said the younger of the two newcomers. "The world never believes—let it pass—'tis no matter. The secret of my birth—" And then the young man shared his mystery. "Gentlemen, I will reveal it to you, for I feel I may have confidence in you. By rights, I am a duke!"

"Jim's eyes bugged out when he heard that," good Huck reports, "and I reckon mine did, too." For it seems the young vagabond they'd just picked up was, by his own admission, the great-great-grandson of none other than the Duke of Bridgewater!

That was when the news got truly surprising, for the older, baldheaded tramp had a secret as well! "Bilgewater," he said to the duke, "kin I trust you?"

"To the bitter death," replied the duke.

"Bilgewater, I am the late Dauphin! . . . Your eyes is lookin' at this very moment on the pore disappeared Dauphin, Looy the Seventeen, son of Looy the Sixteen and Marry Antonette."

Well, what could Huck and Jim do then? Sure, these two itinerant nobles looked like nothing more than traveling bums and con men, yet what if they really were a duke and a king right there on the mighty Mississippi?

Huck reports, "So Jim and I set to majestying him, and doing this and that and t'other for him. . . ." And for Bridgewater as well, the two set about serving him at dinner and calling him "Your Grace," or "My Lord," or "Your Lordship." In all, they treated the duke and the king like, well, a duke and a king. And as you may guess, the nobles liked it so much they stayed on quite a while with Jim and Huck.

And yet for our money (and Mark Twain's as well), the noblest two on that raft weren't the duke and the king, but their "servants" who sacrificed their own comfort for total strangers. For as Huck points out later, "It didn't take me long to make up my mind that these liars warn't no kings nor dukes at all, but just low-down humbugs and frauds. But I never said nothing, never let on; kept it to myself. . .and it warn't no use to tell Jim, so I didn't tell him."

The moral of the story? Well, the next time

you're traveling down the river of life and come across a few people claiming to be nobles, better take a closer look. It just may be the so-called servants who are really dukes and kings.

◆❧

MARK TWAIN—BANKRUPT!

Mark Twain (pen name of Samuel L. Clemens), the author of the classic novel *The Adventures of Huckleberry Finn,* knew something of what it means to live an honorable, noble life. Born in 1835 in Missouri, he lived until 1910 when he died while living in Connecticut. During the time in between, he became famous for his wonderful stories like those of Huck Finn, of Tom Sawyer, and even of a fantastic jumping frog.

Fact is, Mark Twain made a fortune from his writing and lecturing. In fact, he made so much money that he invested substantial amounts of money in, and became director of, the Webster Publishing Company. At age fifty-seven, Mark Twain seemed set for life.

At age fifty-eight, he was bankrupt.

It seems the Webster Publishing Company fell on hard times, finally going under during the panic of 1893–94. Twain's wife had tried to keep the company afloat by giving over $65,000 of her personal inheritance to Webster Publishing

Company, but it just wasn't enough. On April 18, 1894, the publishing company finally succumbed to bankruptcy, leaving behind $94,000 in debt owed to ninety-six different creditors.

At this point, Mark Twain could have simply walked away. As director of Webster Publishing Company, he was not personally liable for the company's debts. He could have shrugged his shoulders, said "Sorry!" and gone on living his life in relative comfort. But he didn't.

Mark Twain sent notices to those ninety-six creditors letting them know a man of honor was behind their loans, and vowing to honor those debts and pay them off—no matter how long it would take. For the next several years, Twain and his family scrimped and saved from their own household budget, allocating the savings to creditors from the Webster Publishing Company. He stepped up his lecturing and his writing, taking every penny possible to pay toward the overwhelming debts.

By the beginning of 1898, less than four years after the bankruptcy, Mark Twain had managed to pay off all $94,000 of the company's debts from his own personal income. He had kept his word, fulfilled an obligation that was not his, and proven to the world that at least one honorable man still lived on this green and blue marble we call home.

Now the question we must ask is this: Do

honorable men and women still reside here on Planet Earth? If we can learn from Mark Twain's example and endeavor to live our lives with honor as he did, then the answer to that question, for as long as we shall live, will always be: "Yes!"

ॐ

Out of the horrendous Columbine High School shooting tragedy in 1999 came this story of how one Christian teenager— Cassie Bernall—faced death with nobility and courage. Her mother, Misty Bernall, recalls that story for you here. . .

She Said Yes*

by Misty Bernall

From what I have since been told, it must have been about eleven-fifteen that morning when Cassie walked into the high school library, back-pack on her shoulder, to do her latest homework assignment—another installment of *Macbeth* for English class. Crystal, a close friend, was in the library, too:

Sara, Seth, and I had just gone over to the library to study, like any other day. We had been there maybe five minutes, when a teacher came running in, yelling that there were kids with guns in the hall. At first we were like, "It's a joke, a senior prank." Seth said, "Relax, it's just paint balls." Then we heard shots, first down the hall, then coming closer and closer. Mrs. Nielsen was yelling at us to get under the tables, but no one listened. Then a kid came in and dropped to the floor. There was blood all over his shoulder. We got under our table, fast. Mrs. Nielsen was at the phone by now, calling 911. Seth was holding me in his arms, with his hand on my head, because I was shaking so badly, and Sara was huddled under there with us, too, holding on to my legs. Then Eric and Dylan came into the library, shooting and saying things like, "We've been waiting to do this our whole lives," and cheering after each shot.

I had no idea who they were—I only found out their names afterward—but their voices sounded scary, evil. At the same time they seemed so happy, like they were playing a game and getting a good kick out of it. Then they came up to our table and knocked a chair over. It hit my arm, and then it hit Sara on the head. They were right above us. I could hardly

*breathe, I was so scared. Then they sud-
denly left the room, probably to reload. It
seemed like they had run out of ammuni-
tion. That's when we ran for it. We
dashed out a side door of the library, an
emergency exit, and made it just before
they came back in.*

Crystal lost track of Cassie once the shooters
entered the room, and there are conflicting ver-
sions of what she was doing. One student remembers seeing her under a table, hands clasped in
prayer; another says she remained seated. Josh, a
sophomore who spoke with me a few weeks after
the incident, did not see her at all, but he says he
will never forget what he heard as he crouched
under a desk about twenty-five feet away:

*I couldn't see anything when those guys
came up to Cassie, but I could recognize
her voice. I could hear everything like it
was right next to me. One of them asked
her if she believed in God. She paused,
like she didn't know what she was going
to answer, and then she said yes. She must
have been scared, but her voice didn't
sound shaky. It was strong. Then they
asked her why, though they didn't give
her a chance to respond. They just blew
her away.*

Josh says that the way the boys questioned Cassie made him wonder whether she was visibly praying.

> I don't understand why they'd pop that question on someone who wasn't. She could've been talking to them, it's hard to tell. I know they were talking the whole time they were in the library. They went over to Isaiah and taunted him. They called him a nigger before they killed him. Then they started laughing and cheering. It was like a big game for them. Then they left the room, so I got up, grabbed my friend Brittany by the hand, and started to run. The next thing I remember is pushing her through the door and flying out after her. . . .

One of the first officials on the scene the next day was Gary, a member of our church and an investigator from the Jefferson County sheriff's department:

> When we got to the school they divided us up into seven teams of investigators. All of the victims who had been killed had been left in place overnight, because the investigators wanted to make sure that everything was documented before they collected the evidence.

As soon as I entered the library I saw Cassie. I knew it was her immediately. She was lying under a table close to another girl. Cassie had been shot in the head at very close range. In fact, the bullet wound indicated that the muzzle was touching her skin. She may have put a hand up to protect herself, because the tip of one finger was blown away, but she couldn't have had time to do more. The blast took her instantly. . . .

The gap between April 20 and the present grows a little wider with every passing day, but the details refuse to fade. Sometimes the images surface so vividly, it seems like it all happened yesterday. Doctors say the brain forgets pain, and that may be so. I am not sure the heart forgets. If there is any reassurance to be found in the recesses of the mind, it may be in those happy, simple things that held us together as a family during the last week of Cassie's life. Though uneventful in themselves, they are strangely satisfying to hang on to, and comforting to replay. . . .

Looking back on the last evening of Cassie's life, I still see her sitting there in the kitchen. She hadn't done her chores yet, and I'm sure I nagged at her. Now that she's gone it's painful to admit. So is my belated recognition that our relationship, though generally good, was not ideal—not that night, nor any other. But it's too late to agonize over what could have been.

Perhaps the cruelest irony of losing Cassie the way we did is the fact that she never would have been at Columbine that day in the first place had we not tried to rescue her by pulling her out of another high school, the one where she had begun the ninth grade, just two-and-a-half years before. Of course, at that time our relationship was frayed almost beyond repair, and it felt like a minor victory every time we got her home from school in one piece, let alone into the kitchen for a mundane event like a family meal or an evening of homework. But that's another chapter.

❧

The King Who Acted Like a King

Chances are you've heard of Emperor Charlemagne (also known as Charles the Great), ruler of much of western Europe during the eighth century A.D. If so, you know that he ruled a huge kingdom—one that he made all the larger through wars and conquests until the Pope eventually crowned him "emperor."

What you might not know is that there was much more to this great king than his political and military prowess. Historians report that Charlemagne was a devoted Christian, that he had memorized so much of the Bible that he could quote Scripture better than many clergymen of his time, and that he had a deep love for the music of the church.

Admirable as those qualities may be, there's one other character quality he possessed that makes Charlemagne a true nobleman in our eyes: his concern for the poor and lowly of his kingdom. During a time when most royalty taxed the poor mercilessly to fund the whims of the rich, Charlemagne did just the opposite—he instituted taxes on the rich and used the money collected to help the poor. (We think Robin Hood would have liked this king!)

But perhaps the best examples of Charlemagne's nobility are revealed in three stories from his personal life.

The first takes place in a proud cathedral in the heart of Charlemagne's empire. While traveling through the country, the emperor and his companions stopped to attend worship services at an ornate church. As things turn out, a poor little monk from the countryside was also traveling and stopped in that self-same church for worship.

The country monk had no idea his emperor was in the congregation; he simply noticed that all the other monks had gathered in the choir section of the church. Dutifully, the little man went up and joined his brothers in the front of the cathedral.

Just after the country churchman had settled into a spot in the choir, the choirmaster gave a signal and all of the other monks immediately began a choral chant they'd memorized for the occasion! The wandering monk jumped in surprise, then felt his face go red because he had no idea how to chant like his brothers were, or what words to chant along with them.

The choirmaster noticed the outsider immediately, and knowing Emperor Charlemagne himself was in the audience, determined to do something. So the choirmaster carefully moved toward the new monk, raised his baton, and spat out these words, "If you do not open your mouth and sing, I am going to hit you!"

Now the little monk felt truly trapped. He couldn't sneak away, and he definitely didn't want to get smacked by the choirmaster's baton, so he did the only thing he could think to do: He opened and closed his mouth repeatedly, hoping it looked like he was singing the chant along with the others. But of course, it didn't. Before long, there were snickers in the congregation. Then guffaws. Then outright laughter at the humiliation of the little monk. And the harder he tried, the more the audience laughed at the little man.

But one member of the congregation remained serene, refusing to join in the jeering laughter that surrounded him. Emperor Charlemagne simply kept his seat in watchful silence as the little comedy unfolded before him. After the worship service, the Emperor leaned forward and called for the embarrassed country monk to come forward.

The monk was devastated, certain he was in for a tongue-lashing—or worse—from the great king. But Charlemagne simply smiled peacefully and said, "My good monk, I just wanted to thank you for, uh, all your efforts at singing today."

Next, Charlemagne commanded his men to give the poor monk a pound of silver to further show the king's appreciation. The monk's smile soon broadened to match that of his king, for in one fell swoop, the Emperor had salvaged the poor man's dignity and made him the envy of all those who only moments before had laughed him to scorn.

Another time, while at his home church, Charlemagne waited for another group of monks to begin their singing chants—but one church-man was missing from the choir. It was a prominent monk that Charlemagne had just promoted to the office of bishop within the church! The newly made bishop had been so proud of his new office that he'd spent lavishly on a feast and wine, and by the time of the church service he was so drunk and stuffed with food he lay drowsing at home, muttering occasionally, "Gran' day. Gran' day indeed!"

Thus the moment came for this drunken

monk to chant his solo for the Emperor—and he was not there! At that moment the rest of the monks in the choir all fell silent, unsure what to do without their soloist present. They began to poke at each other, saying, "You chant his part!" "No, you chant it!"

Finally Charlemagne had had enough. "Come on now," he roared from the congregation. "One of you must chant it!"

At last, one lowly little monk stepped forward. He was not one who was good at his studies—in fact, he was rather looked down upon by his comrades in the monastery. But when he heard the Emperor's request, he determined to obey—and he was awful! His nervousness only added to his lack of education, and his shaky little voice obviously didn't know the part at all. A panicked look spread over his face and he must've thought to himself, *Oh dear, what have I done!?!*

Suddenly the roar returned from the audience as Charlemagne commanded, "You others! Help him out!" The other voices swelled around the wavering monk's voice, and mercifully, they all finished the song together.

Next morning the erstwhile soloist heard a knock at his door. It was one of Charlemagne's servants commanding the lowly monk to appear before the king! Frightened nearly out of his wits, the monk hurriedly made his way to the Emperor.

Charlemagne surveyed him quietly for a moment, then spoke. "Who told you to sing that part?" he said, referring to the botched solo the day before.

Stammering, the monk bowed and replied, "M-my lord, you said someone must sing."

The emperor asked a few more questions about the monk's performance the prior day. Then, taking the lowly, frightened man, they went together to meet with the king's nobles. There, Charlemagne announced, "A certain proud man, whom I just appointed bishop, apparently has no respect or honor for me or God. He couldn't put off his party even long enough to chant the music assigned to him. Therefore, he shall not be the new bishop."

The king turned to the frightened monk at his side and smiled. "You shall be my new bishop instead. That is what God wants and what I want. Now try and do a good job."

Once again, the king had opposed the proud and lifted up the humble, a noble act indeed.

The last story of Emperor Charlemagne we will share with you today is also our favorite. Seems the king was again at a church service where a young relative of his sang "Alleluia" for the congregation. Afterward, Charlemagne commented to the bishop of that church, "That young man of ours certainly sang well!"

The bishop, not having met the young singer,

thought he was simply a young "nobody" and not worth the bishop's time. So the clergyman sniffed out this withering reply, "Oh yes. That's just how the country bumpkins drone when they're out following the oxen that pull the plow."

Charlemagne couldn't stand for anyone so arrogant to insult the young lad, so he did what no other nobleman would have dared to do. He decked him. Knocked the bishop flat on the ground and walked away!

And as far as we're concerned, that was exactly the "noble act" that bishop deserved.

❧

THE NOBLE AWARDS

These days there are awards of all kinds. Awards for running fast and awards for jumping high, awards for making movies and awards for singing songs, awards for being the most fashionable and even awards for those who demonstrate their lack of fashion. The list goes on and on. So why not create an award of your own? Call it The Noble Award, and present it to those you see doing noble acts.

First, you'll need an actual award. Perhaps you have a high-tech computer with nifty software and can make a professional-looking certificate. Or you might have artistic ability to draw a lovely award on parchment paper or sculpt a few tiny figures from wood or clay. Your Noble Award might even be a monetary gift, a certificate for dinner or a shopping spree, or a large platter of cookies. You decide.

Then you'll need a list of nominees. Think of those unsung heroes in your home, your community, your church, your workplace. What about the garbage collectors who faithfully remove your stinky trash each week? Or the secretary at your child's school who does everything from running off copies to making phone calls to applying Band-Aids. How about the nursery workers who faithfully change diapers, wipe noses, and rock infants week after week? Consider all those who seem to be quietly doing the tasks no one else wants to do—yet that must be done by someone.

Now you need a ceremony. You might want to serve dessert in your home and invite the nominees. Or plan a special party in honor of the nominees. Or post a notice of a quick meeting to be held at work around the time everyone plans his or her coffee break. No tuxedos are required, but you'll need a time and place to make your presentation.

Finally, present the awards. Regale everyone present with the many reasons these people deserve awards. Applaud them all, bring out The Nobles, then give an award to each nominee! They certainly deserve it!

AMERICAN NOBILITY

Pop Quiz! Take this little test to see if you can spot America's true nobility:

1. True or false: A United States senator is more important to your life than your local garbage collector.
2. True or false: A movie star makes a bigger difference in your life than your favorite pet (dog, cat, etc.).
3. True or false: The president of the U.S.A. cares more about you than your parents.
4. True or false: Your boss at work adds more value to your life than your children.
5. True or false: Your child's favorite sports hero makes a bigger difference on the child's future than his or her fourth-grade teacher.
6. True or false: The manager of the nicest restaurant in town is more vital to your family's daily life than is the produce stocker at your local grocery store.
7. True or false: It's a higher privilege to shake the governor's hand than it is to shake your pastor's hand.

Not sure how to answer the questions in this quiz? Think of it this way then: Which of those above would be the hardest for you to live without? They are America's true nobility, for they have the most impact on your life.

Now, isn't it time you and I treated them as such?

SPEAKING OF NOBILITY. . .

"The most ennobling experience in life is the awareness that one is an instrument of deity being used to further His purpose on the earth."
A. P. GOUTHEY,
as quoted by ALFRED MONTAPERT in
Words of Wisdom to Live By

"Each time a man stands up for an ideal, or acts to improve the lot of others, or strikes out against injustice, he sends forth a tiny ripple of hope. . . and crossing each other from a million different centers of energy and daring, those ripples build a current that can sweep down the mightiest walls of oppression and resistance."
ROBERT KENNEDY,
as quoted by CHARLES HENNING in
The Wit and Wisdom of Politics

"What is the use of living if it be not to strive for noble causes and to make this muddled world a better place for those who will live in it after we are gone?"
WINSTON CHURCHILL,
in a 1908 speech to the
Scottish Liberal Association

*"I am going to help my Gram-Gram.
She is the one who taught me,
'It is better to be truthful and good, than to not.'"*
Con man FREDDY BENSON
(portrayed by Steve Martin), in
Dirty Rotten Scoundrels

"Character cannot be developed in ease and quiet.
Only through experience of trial and suffering
can the soul be strengthened, ambition inspired,
and success achieved." HELEN KELLER,
in *Helen Keller's Journal*

"In our lives we will encounter many challenges,
and tomorrow we face one together. How we
accept the challenge and attack the challenge head
on is only about us—no one can touch that. If we
win or lose this weekend, it will not make a difference in our lives. But why we play and how we
play will make a difference in our lives forever."
BETH ANDERS,
as quoted by GEORGE HETZEL, JR.,
in *The Coaches' Little Playbook*

"The ultimate foundation of the value and dignity of man, of the meaning of his life, is the fact
that he is God's image and likeness!"
POPE JOHN PAUL II,
in *Fear Not*

"In great deeds something abides. On great fields something stays. Forms change and pass; bodies disappear; but spirits linger. . . . This is the great reward of service, to give life's best for such high stake that it shall be found again unto life eternal."

JOSHUA LAWRENCE CHAMBERLAIN,
reflecting on the end of America's Civil War,
as quoted in *Brink of Destruction*

"The first prayer I want my son to learn to say for me is not 'God keep Daddy safe' but 'God make Daddy brave, and if he has hard things to do, make him strong to do them.' Life and death don't matter, my son. Right and wrong do. Daddy dead is Daddy still, but Daddy dishonored before God is something awful, too bad for words."

World War I chaplain
GEOFFREY STUDDERT KENNEDY,
in a letter to his son, as quoted by
R. KENT HUGHES in
1001 Great Stories and Quotes

"I have a dream that one day on the red hills of Georgia, sons of former slaves and sons of former slave-owners will be able to sit down together at the table of brotherhood. I have a dream that one day, even the state of Mississippi, a state sweltering in the heat of injustice, sweltering with the heat of oppression, will be transformed into an oasis of freedom and justice. I have a dream my four little

children will one day live in a nation where they will not be judged by the color of their skin, but by the content of their character. I have a dream today!"   REV. MARTIN LUTHER KING, JR.,
in the speech, *I Have a Dream*

❧

THE WORD ON NOBILITY. . .

A wife of noble character who can find?
She is worth far more than rubies.
PROVERBS 31:10 NIV

He has shown you, O man, what is good; And what does the LORD require of you but to do justly, to love mercy, and to walk humbly with your God?   MICAH 6:8 NKJV

Do not be misled:
"Bad company corrupts good character."
1 CORINTHIANS 15:33 NIV

"Now don't worry about a thing, my daughter. I will do what is necessary, for everyone in town knows you are an honorable woman."

RUTH 3:11 NLT

But the noble man devises noble plans;
And by noble plans he stands.
ISAIAH 32:8 NASB

As they discovered in 1861 in Parkville, Colorado, sometimes the most honorable thing we can do is to preserve someone else's honor! Read on to discover what happened. . .

A Matter of Honor

Tempers ran hot in Parkville, Colorado, when the American Civil War broke out in 1861. Residents of this booming little mining town hailed from both the North and the South, and one fateful day a Southern Rebel got into an argument about the war with a Northern-bred Yankee. Before long the two men had insulted each other's honor and, as was the custom of that time, had vowed to settle the matter through a gun duel.

Each man chose a "Second"—an assistant in the duel. The Seconds carefully loaded a pair of revolvers for the battle and recruited other armed men to stand ready in case one of the combatants cheated. If either dueler fired his weapon before the count of three, those additional armed men would shoot the cheater dead.

Finally the town doctor was called on hand, and the Reb and the Yank prepared for the duel. Each man faced the other and held opposite ends of a handkerchief in one hand, thus keeping them at close range and preventing either from running away from his foe's bullets. In their opposite hands each man held the loaded revolvers their Seconds had prepared.

The count began. "One!" Sweat appeared on the face of the Rebel. "Two!" The handkerchief hand of the Yankee trembled just a little. Silence ruled the moment. Everyone expected both men to be dead soon after the count of three.

"Three!"

Without hesitation, both guns fired at point-blank range. Both men fell backward to the floor, bullet holes burned in their shirts. The doctor rushed to examine one body, then the next. Instead of gushing wounds, all he found were red welts on each man's stomach.

Suddenly, the truth was known. The Seconds, in their own little conspiracy, had loaded each weapon with wax bullets! Feeling incomparable relief, the Yankee and the Rebel finally stood up as uncontrollable laughter gushed from their lips and soon overtook nearly everyone in the room. Finally, the two combatants shook hands and parted amiably, agreeing to disagree.

The Seconds walked away, too, content in the knowledge that with a little clever thinking they'd each preserved a friend's honor—and his life as well.

❧

Many years ago, Mike's mother, Zahea Nappa, left an indelible lesson about honor in the mind of her young son. Read on to hear Mike explain that lesson in his own words here. . .

HONOR AMONG THIEVES

One thing I remember from my younger days is being hungry. Now, that's not to suggest that I or my three sisters were neglected and starved as children, but the truth is that we were very poor growing up. For an active young boy like myself, that meant there was often not enough food to satisfy the seemingly constant gnawing in my stomach.

We laugh about them now, but the stories of having nothing to eat for days but a bag of pinto beans and a can of hominy grits were all too true. I remember being thrilled the day a government truck pulled up in front of our home with blocks of cheese for the poor, or when the ice-cream man felt sorry for us kids and gave us each a cold treat from his truck. I remember being embarrassed to be on the "free lunch" program at my elementary school, but I also knew that on some days that free lunch would be my only meal.

My mother worked hard during those days. A single mother of four children, she worked two and three jobs at a time, and managed to earn her doctorate from the University of Oklahoma as well—something we all hoped would lead to a better-paying job and more money for our family.

Finally, it came. Imagine our excitement when Mom came home with the news that she'd landed a new job with a big fat paycheck attached! She'd be working for a company I'll call Brain, Inc., serving clients all over the country—and best of all, earning what we'd always thought our mom was worth anyway (or at least close to it).

After the paychecks started coming in, I remember smiling and pausing just to take it all in when I found our refrigerator full of food after school one day. Mom also bought us other things we'd been needing, like new shoes and clothes, and even a few treats like dinner in a restaurant or two. It seemed we were finally on the way up. Our financial woes would soon be over.

Then one day my mother left town to go on a business trip for Brain, Inc. She hired a friend to stay with us kids while she was gone and went on her way. A few days later she was home again, unexpectedly early.

Her face was grim, but confident. "Well, kids," she said after gathering us together in the living room. "I'm going to have to find a new job, because I'm no longer working for Brain, Inc. I quit."

We were shocked, and all I remember thinking was that I'd better get used to being hungry again. Then she told us what had happened on her trip.

"They wanted me to lie," she said. "They told me to tell a customer something that just wasn't true in order to make the sale. I told my boss I wouldn't do it, that I couldn't face my kids knowing I'd lost my integrity. He told me I'd better lie or I'd lose my job." She shrugged as if it were an easy decision. "So I quit, and caught the next plane back home."

We were poor once again, but I've never been more proud of my mother. When faced with a choice between necessity and honor, she chose to be honorable—and taught me a lesson about character at the same time.

It's been decades since our family experience with Brain, Inc., but I've often remembered my mother's courage at that time. In fact, twice in my life I've been placed in situations similar to hers. And both times I've said to myself, "I know what Mom would do," and I walked away. Funny thing is, both times God brought along for me new jobs that eventually paid me at least double the previous ones—and allowed me to continue striving to be a man of good character.

What else could I do, really? After all, if being a person of honor is good enough for my momma, it's good enough for me.

Ten Noble Acts
You Can Do Today

1. Love your children—and let them know it.
2. Invest in your relationship with God by reading your Bible and praying.
3. Honor your parent(s) by writing a letter of thanks for all they've invested in your life.
4. Vote.
5. Donate time, money, or materials to your favorite charity.
6. Donate time, money, or materials to your local church.
7. Serve a server, such as your pastor, a police officer, a nursery worker, or another by offering to wash a car, rake leaves, mow a lawn, run errands, or do some other mundane chore everyone must do.
8. Be an example of honesty and integrity for your children.
9. Lead your family in learning about God.
10. Imitate Jesus all day long.

in silent salute as we pass by. A cow wanders behind him, her copper bell softly clanging.

After a few wrong turns, we reach our destination: a farmhouse rebuilt with funding from The Salvation Army. When they hear us arrive, the whole family pours out of the house: mom, dad, kids, and grandparents. We greet each other and admire the new roof and all the repairs. Chickens dart at our feet, clucking and cackling, while kittens play tag nearby in the sweet green grass. Roger Markic, who co-directs The Salvation Army's micro-enterprise program and is also our translator, supplies the words that the family's grateful smiles only hint at.

They invite us in for thick Turkish coffee and slivovitz, a homemade plum brandy. Declining the brandy, we thank them for the coffee and join them inside. Their living room is plain: the floors are wood, a bare light bulb dangles from the ceiling, and a wood-burning stove radiates warmth from the corner. On the windowsill, knitting needles hold a pair of beige wool socks, not yet complete. I look out the window and see the most beautiful valley on earth.

The patriarch, sixty-seven-year-old Rakita Ilija, thoughtfully recounts the rich agricultural heritage of the area, devastated during the war. His family used to be rich, he says. Before the war came to Sipovo, they had five cows, one hundred sheep, a tractor, a horse, and an electric mill to grind the wheat. When they returned, all their livestock was gone. Later, they found the bones of the bull in the yard.

Yet, he says, "When we returned, we cried for joy to see our home. Everyone wants to come home to die. Generations of our family lived here. My father died last month at 100 or 110—who knows?—he was born here."

I sit silently and wonder at his hope and perseverance. For days I've seen buildings that were riddled with bullet holes, heard stories of death and devastation, photographed the remains of homes swallowed up in ashes and rubble, and talked to victims of the war as tears ran down my cheeks.

I look at Roger and think of his house, where we visited yesterday. It's in a beautiful spot with hills all around, a lovely vegetable garden, and chickens in a pen. The stone walls are being repaired, and the red tile roof has been replaced.

But inside, the rubble remains—mute testimony to the angry fire that burned the roof and destroyed the inside of the house. Roger and his father are slowly clearing it out and repairing the damage. Despite the charred timbers, twisted electrical wires, and empty windows, I know it was once warm, charming, and filled with love. I can picture the lace curtains, the familiar conversations, and the laughter.

And I wonder: *What do they do with their*

anger? Where is the rage? How does it feel to shovel out the ashes and rubble of your life's dreams, to be the victim of a war you did not want, the victim of another's hatred?

I think about the rage and anger with each house I photograph, each person I talk to. Finally, I muster my courage and ask Branslav Lujic, who also lost his house, how he deals with his pain.

I find comfort in his words. "People couldn't survive if they always think about the war," he explains; "it would be too much. As I repair my house I think of other things. I think that to-morrow is a new day."

Often, it isn't easy to do the right thing, but as Jodi Jantomaso learned, it is always worth it. . .

HER NAME WAS GRACE*

"Grace Miller, R.N." the name badge said. She was a nurse, a woman in her mid-fifties with short curly hair who worked at the Boca Raton, Florida, medical clinic where Jodi Jantomaso went for health care. Though the two had never really met, Grace always greeted Jodi with a warm smile and a wave whenever Jodi came into the office.

But that spring Friday in 1988 Jodi didn't notice whether or not Grace was on duty. She had other things on her mind—mainly her 2:00 P.M. abortion appointment that same afternoon. Jodi had arrived at the clinic at 10:00 A.M. for the preliminary bloodwork and preparations. Now she sat in the waiting room, feeling helpless and afraid.

She hadn't intended for things to work out this way. Only twenty-seven years old, she'd already been through a painful divorce and had—until recently—been very much in love with a man named Michael. They'd met at the posh resort in Boca Raton where Jodi worked managing the spa and fitness facility. Young, fit, and attractive, she'd quickly caught Michael's eye at the spa. He also was handsome, as well as wealthy and fun to be around. It wasn't long before they were dating. Soon after, Jodi moved in with Michael so they could be together more.

"Spiritually, I was at a low point," Jodi admits now. Turning her back on what she knew God wanted, she chose to pursue happiness in the form of her lover, Michael. Together they talked of marriage, children, and living happily ever after.

While Michael was away on a business trip, Jodi found out she was pregnant. She was so excited about telling him the good news! He was to return on February 14, 1988, so Jodi planned a special Valentine's surprise to reveal to him that he would be a father.

When he walked in the door on Valentine's Day, he seemed distracted, or tired, or both. Jodi was nearly bursting with excitement. She handed him a gift, a baby's rattle she'd wrapped to clue him in to the pregnancy.

"He opened the rattle, looked at me and said. . .nothing. I said, 'We're having a baby!' He got up from the table, looked at me, and said, 'Well, things have changed now.'"

And then he dropped the bombshell. While on his business trip, he'd decided to leave Jodi for another woman, his attorney, Maria. He spoke to Jodi as if the matter were settled. "You'll need to do something about this. Soon."

The next days and weeks were a blur, until the moment Jodi found herself, nervous, numb, and alone, sitting in a doctor's office waiting for the time when she'd abort the child growing in her womb. *Oh, God, what am I supposed to do now?* she'd sobbed time and again during the recent days. But God wasn't listening. Or so it seemed.

Before the actual abortion, the doctor wanted to do a preparatory ultrasound. She turned on the equipment and soon was looking at a fuzzy black image of the inside of Jodi's womb. Suddenly, desperately, Jodi wanted to see what the doctor was seeing. She asked to look at the ultrasound monitor screen. At first the doctor refused, but when Jodi insisted, the doctor repositioned the screen to allow her a brief glimpse.

Jodi gazed at the near-incomprehensible picture and saw something blinking in the X-ray-like blackness. "What's that?" she asked.

"The heartbeat," the doctor replied matter-of-factly.

Jodi was stunned. Tears immediately sprang from her eyes. "I'd been so naïve about everything!" she says. "This wasn't just a fetus; it was a live baby!" With that knowledge came a new resolve. Jodi instantly got up from the table, cancelled her appointment, got dressed, and went outside where she sat on the sidewalk, crying.

Oh, God, what am I supposed to do now?

she silently sobbed again.

Then Jodi felt someone standing next to her. She looked up and saw the name badge: "Grace Miller, R.N."

The kind nurse put a hand on the young woman's shoulder and spoke. "Jodi, you've made the right choice," she said. "God is going to bless you and your baby, and use you more than you could imagine. He'll always provide for you both."

The nurse's words were like a breath of fresh air, and Jodi clung to them like oxygen, desperate for the hope they offered. Grateful for the encouragement, Jodi thanked the nurse, tried to dry her eyes, and went to her car to drive home.

Michael was enraged. He tried everything to get Jodi to change her mind, even offering her an envelope containing $20,000 in cash if Jodi would abort the child. Remembering Grace's words, she refused.

September 29, 1988, Jodi Jantomaso gave birth to a beautiful baby girl, Joelle Aleece. Returning to her Christian roots, Jodi became involved in church again, and when Joelle was only two years old the little girl joined her mother in singing and performing for their delighted congregation.

Several years after that, Jodi met and fell in love with a Christian musician, Eric Jaqua. They married, and now all three—Jodi, Eric, and Joelle—are involved in speaking and performing for churches and charities nationwide. Inspired by "Grace Miller, R.N.," they also invest their time in ministering to women who, like Jodi, find themselves in a crisis pregnancy situation.

The story doesn't end there, though. In 1995 Jodi and Joelle went back to that medical clinic in Boca Raton, hoping to look up Grace Miller and thank her in person for helping Jodi to choose life.

But Grace Miller wasn't there. A look at the payroll records from 1988 revealed that no Grace Miller had worked at the clinic. Unbelieving, Jodi asked to speak with her former doctor at the facility. Thankfully, the doctor remembered Jodi and came out to greet her.

Jodi explained the situation. To her surprise, the doctor shook her head and said, "There's never been anyone by the name of Grace who's ever worked here."

Then Jodi realized that God was listening when she cried to Him for help so many years before. In response, He'd sent an angel of comfort—one appropriately named Grace—to bring hope and courage to Jodi for a few brief, critical moments. And by doing that, He had saved both a child and a mother at the same time.

"Grace left such an impression on me," Jodi says today. "She touched me by her kindness and words—words from God for me. They're never forgotten."

A Father/Son Lesson on Business Ethics

The classic joke goes something like this. . .

A young man was taking a class in business ethics and was having trouble understanding his homework on rights and wrongs of business dealings. His father, owner of the local hardware store, soon came to his aid.

"Son," the dad said, "it's like this. Imagine a customer comes into my store to buy a hundred-dollar sander, and he pays for it with a shiny new hundred-dollar bill. As he walks out of the store and toward his car, I suddenly notice that he gave me not one, but two hundred-dollar bills by mistake. The bills were so new, they'd simply stuck together.

"Now it becomes an issue of right or wrong in business. At this point I must ask myself: Should I tell my partner?"

A Code to Live By*

*by Christopher D. Hudson,
Denise Kohlmeyer, and Randy Southern*

What if someone asked you to write down your own personal code of ethics? Could you do it? Could you come up with a list of, say, six principles, ideals, or rules that govern your life and your business dealings? Six absolutes. Six statements of what you believe to be right and wrong.

Many people take a passive approach to right and wrong. They have no strong feelings about either one. As a result, when they're faced with a tempting situation—at work or anywhere—they have no strong principles to guide them. And in many instances they make regrettable decisions.

The business world is crawling with un-scrupulous characters, people with plans and schemes to get ahead at any cost. Do you know the type? If not, you will. Someday they may use you in one of their plans. They may give you an opportunity for some serious cash or career recognition. All you'll have to do is "play along." And if you have no strong feelings about right or wrong, you might be tempted to do just that—at the risk of your reputation and your career.

Bad influences are just half of the story. If it were only "bad guys" you had to watch out for, corporate life wouldn't be such a minefield of ethical crises. After all, even the smoothest vil-lains eventually show their true colors.

What you need to watch out for are the seemingly harmless everyday situations that catch you off guard or with your defenses down and cause you to consider things that are otherwise completely out of character for you. Those are the situations that can get you into trouble faster than anything.

We're not suggesting that writing a code of ethics is somehow going to magically protect you from the temptations of the business of the business world. It will, however, give you a chance to think about the values that are closest to your heart and the principles that mean the most to you.

If you're still unsure about writing your own code of ethics, at least take a look at the ethical standards we've listed on the pages that follow. How many of them seem like sound principles to you, things you might include in your own code of ethics (if you had one)? Which ones seem a bit extreme to you? Which ones would never work in a business setting? Which ones are hopelessly outdated in today's high-tech, high-pressure culture?

Here are six ethical statements, each of which has a specific application for the business sector. How many of them would you be willing to apply to your career?

1. I will maintain the highest standards of integrity in dealing with clients and coworkers.

   Integrity is an all-encompassing word that suggests a moral basis beyond ethics, a deep-seated sense of right and wrong that governs every aspect of a person's life. Integrity is a proactive attribute, not a reactive one. For example, a person with ethics would recognize when he is facing a serious temptation and react appropriately. A person with integrity would avoid situations that might present a temptation. To put it another way, people with integrity do not put themselves in compromising positions.

2. I will deal fairly with everyone, giving due respect to the opinions of others.

Fairness is treating people in an appropriate manner, avoiding both favoritism and discrimination. Giving due respect to a person's opinion does not mean you have to agree with that opinion. It means that you show the person the courtesy of considering what he has to say. Of the six ethical statements, this one is probably the easiest to violate unwittingly. Think about it: How many people's opinions do you fail to respect every day? If you're like the rest of us, you'll find that the answer it "quite a few." If you recognize that you've failed to treat someone fairly or respect someone's opinion, apologize to that person and set the situation right at your earliest opportunity.

3. I will adhere to highest standards of accuracy and truth.

Journalists, reporters, and tabloid editors, please step to the front for this presentation. Truth telling is fast becoming a lost art in corporate America. One of the best dodges for telling the truth is hiding behind legal mumbo jumbo. The prevailing attitude is that it's not wrong unless you can be sued for it. The ethical position is that if it's not the truth, an accurate representation of the facts, it should not be presented as such. In an office setting, that would include taking credit for someone else's work, inflating budgets, or making extravagant claims.

4. I will not knowingly spread false or misleading information.

   Obviously, this covers gossip and lying. It could also apply to the questionable practice of quoting "unnamed sources." Take responsibility not only for your actions, but for your words. Don't say anything that you would be ashamed to take credit for later. If you find that you have unwittingly spread false information, act promptly to correct your mistake.

5. I will strictly maintain the secrets and privacy of my clients and coworkers.

   If information is power, privileged information is ultimate power. In the course of your business dealings, you will likely become privileged to know some very personal information about your clients and perhaps even your coworkers. That privileged information can become a source of temptation under the right circumstances. You will likely face situations in which divulging that information could benefit you, perhaps by getting you in good with the boss or making you the center of attention at a party. This is a temptation that must be withstood at all costs. To reveal personal information about someone, under any circumstances, demonstrates a disturbing lack of self-control and untrustworthiness.

6. I will not intentionally damage the reputation of a client, coworker, or competitor.

Think of the sleazy campaign ads you see every election year ("My opponent hasn't paid a dime of child support in the past nine years!" "My opponent allowed a child killer to be released from prison!"). In the heat of battle, people tend to grab for anything that will damage their opponent. You may not have any "opponents" in your career, but chances are you have competitors, people vying with you for clients, promotions, or the respect of peers. And in the heat of competition, you may be tempted to question someone's reputation or repeat a damaging allegation. Don't do it, even if those tactics are being used against you. Stay above the fray. Compete hard, but fairly.

To those of you who choose to draw up your own code of ethics: good for you! When questionable situations arise, you may find yourself pulling out your code for consultation. Don't allow yourself to dismiss your ethical standards. Ask yourself this question: "What's the worst that could happen to me if I follow my code of ethics?" Then ask, "What's the worst that could happen if I ignore my ethical standards?" One word of caution here: Just because you have a code of ethics doesn't mean that you need to impose your standards on your coworkers. Never be shy to share what you believe; but do it in a nonjudgmental way, or you may damage your relationship with your coworkers. Humility is the key. Remember, you're not Moses descending from Mount Sinai with the Ten Commandments inscribed in stone. You're a worker in corporate America just trying to build a career and do what's right (though not necessarily in that order).

๑๏

Twenty-Six Ways to
Right a Wrong This Week

Apologize
Beware of your own biases
Call your mother
Defend the innocent
Empathize
Forgive
Give your time
Help someone in need
Invite God into your relationships with
      people
Just do it
Kindle kindness
Laugh with friends
Make amends
Notice the good in your children
Open your eyes
Pray for forgiveness
Quit making excuses
Refuse to lie
Send chocolate
Telephone your father
Use your talents to support a godly cause
Visit prisoners in jail
Welcome suggestions
X-ray your motives
Yawn at indifference
Zap away prejudice

Speaking of What's Right. . .

"We must use time wisely and forever realize that the time is always ripe to do right."
NELSON MANDELA,
as recorded on Quoteland.com

"If a woman has to choose between catching a fly ball and saving an infant's life, she will choose to save the infant's life without even considering if there are men on base."
Comedian DAVE BARRY,
as quoted by Adam Christing in
Comedy Comes Clean 2

"It is never right to compromise with dishonesty."
HENRY CABOT LODGE, JR.,
as quoted in *The Book of Wisdom*

"I often use a quote by Edward Everett Hale which best sums up my philosophy, 'I am only one, but I am still one. I cannot do everything, but I can still do something. And because I cannot do everything, I will not refuse to do the something I can do.' If everyone would take this to heart, most of our problems would be solved and there would be no need for organizations such as Mothers Against Drunk Driving."
CANDACE LIGHTNER,
founder of Mothers Against Drunk Driving,
as quoted by LORNE A. ADRAIN in
The Most Important Thing I Know

"Always do right—
this will gratify some and astonish the rest."
MARK TWAIN,
in a 1901 speech to
the Young People's Society

"When you know you're right,
you don't care what others think.
You know sooner or later
it will come out in the wash."
BARBARA MCCLINTOCK,
as quoted in *Time* magazine

"You have much more power when you are working for the right thing than when you are working against the wrong thing."

PEACE PILGRIM, in
Peace Pilgrim:
Her Life and Work in Her Own Words

"Morality, including political morality, has to do
with the definition of right conduct, and this is
not simply by way of the ends of action. How we
do what we do is as important as our goals."

PAUL RAMSEY, in
War and the Christian Conscience

"I've seen hate on the faces of too many White
Citizen Councilors in the South to want to hate,
myself, because every time I see it, I know that it

does something to their faces and their personalities and I say to myself that hate is too great a burden to bear. I have decided to love."

REV. MARTIN LUTHER KING, JR.,
as quoted by JIM HASKINS in
*I Have a Dream: The Life and
Words of Martin Luther King, Jr.*

THE WORD ON WHAT'S RIGHT. . .

The LORD is good and right;
he points sinners to the right way.
PSALM 25:8 NCV

Happy are those who don't listen to the wicked, who don't go where sinners go, who don't do what evil people do. They love the LORD's teachings, and they think about those teachings day and night. They are strong, like a tree planted by a river. Psalm 1:1–3 NCV

Do not let any part of your body become a tool of wickedness, to be used for sinning. Instead, give yourselves completely to God since you have been given new life. And use your whole body as a tool to do what is right for the glory of God. Romans 6:13 NLT

I was young and now I am old,
yet I have never seen the righteous forsaken
or their children begging bread.
PSALM 37:25 NIV

All Scripture is inspired by God and is useful to teach us what is true and to make us realize what is wrong in our lives. It straightens us out and teaches us to do what is right.

2 Timothy 3:16 NLT

❧

MODERN-DAY ZACCHAEUS

In Luke 19:1–9, the Scriptures tell us about a tax collector named Zacchaeus and how one encounter with Christ changed his entire life. In fact, it so changed him that afterward Zacchaeus vowed to make right the crookedness of his past by repaying four times the amount he had previously stolen by overcharging people on their taxes.

Perhaps inspired by Zacchaeus, or more likely just changed in heart and mind by his own encounter with Christ, one African Christian determined to make right the crookedness of his past as well. And so, this modern-day Zacchaeus placed an ad in *The East Africa Standard* in Nairobi, Kenya. It read like this:

All Debts to Be Paid

I, *Allan Alia Waniek Harangui*, of P.O. Box 40380, Nairobi, have dedicated my services to the Lord Jesus Christ. I must put right all my wrongs. If I owe you any debt or damage personally or any of the companies I have been director or partner of, i.e.,

Guaranteed Services, Ltd.

Waterpumps Electrical and General, Co.

Sales and Service, Ltd.

Please contact me or my advocates J. L. Kibicho and Company, Advocates, P.O. Box 73137, Nairobi, for a settlement. No amount will be disputed.

God and His Son Jesus Christ be glorified.

A Prayer for Right Living

Author Unknown

Oh, God—when I have food,
Help me to remember the hungry;
When I have work,
Help me to remember the jobless;
When I have a warm home,
Help me to remember the homeless;
When I am without pain,

Help me to remember those who suffer;
And remembering,
Help me destroy my complacency,
And bestir my compassion.
Make me concerned enough to help,
By word and deed, those who cry out—
For what we take for granted.

*Once again, our friend and fellow author,
John Duckworth, has managed to master-
fully illustrate the danger of a life lived
without regard to right or wrong—and to
make us laugh at the same time. So, with
his permission, we've decided to end this
chapter with his humorous—and
thought-provoking—story. . .*

THE NEW UMP*

by John Duckworth

The crowd was going crazy. The score stood at
eight to seven by the start of the ninth inning,
and even the hot dog vendors were starting to
turn from their hawking to watch the championship battle on the diamond. Hats, paper cups,
and souvenir programs bobbed in the air as the
evenly divided spectators cheered their teams

toward victory.

The umpire, a white-haired veteran whose eyes twinkled behind his face mask, whisked dust from home plate as the visiting team took the field. He was about to yell, "Play ball!" when something happened.

"Attention," said an official-sounding voice over the public-address system. "Umpire substitution."

"What?" asked several people in the stands. "What did he say?"

"Umpire substitution," repeated the voice. "The old umpire will be replaced for the remainder of the game."

"Replace him?" a fan cried. "Why? He's done a great job all these years. He's called 'em fairly today, too."

But all the voice would say was, "New ump, please take your position."

With that, a new umpire took his place behind home plate. He looked like the old umpire —same dark blue chest pad, same black pants, same white hair. But he was different somehow.

"You're out," the new ump told his predecessor, jerking a thumb toward the showers. The old umpire shook his head sadly at the crowd, then walked slowly toward the stadium exit.

"Play ball!" the new ump shouted, and players took their positions. The crowd, forgetting its momentary puzzlement, resumed yelling and throwing things.

The pitcher wound up, then let a curve ball fly over the plate. The batter didn't move. Everyone waited for the new ump to yell, "Strike!" but he said nothing.

"Well?" the batter asked impatiently. "Was it a strike or a ball?" Players and spectators watched curiously as the new ump scratched his chin.

"Well, that all depends," the umpire said. "I'd hate to set myself up as a judge, after all." Everyone stared as he meticulously swept off the plate again.

"Wait a minute," cried the coach of the home team, leaping from his bench. "Are you trying to tell me you can't decide whether that ball was a ball or a strike? The old ump could have decided!"

The new ump frowned. "That's precisely why we had to get rid of him," he said. "The old ump was helplessly out of date, always imposing his beliefs on others. He acted as though everything were black or white—a strike or a ball, a safe or an out. Times have changed; we modern people know better."

"We do?" the other coach asked.

"Of course," the new ump said. "These are gray areas. One man's safe is another man's out. Now, play ball—please."

Confused, the players and coaches took their places again. Once more the pitcher wound up and threw—this time a fastball. The batter swung and connected with a loud crack.

"A base hit!" cried the home coach as his half of the crowd cheered.

"No way!" the other coach declared as the ball hit the ground. "It's a foul!"

The coaches approached each other, fists clenched, and for ten minutes bellowed their debate. Finally one of them said hoarsely, "Let's ask the umpire."

"Oh, my," the ump said, pressing his fingertips together thoughtfully. "Who's to say what's foul and what isn't? I certainly can't. The courts come up with a definition. In some countries, what's foul is fair, and what's fair is—"

"I know a foul when I see it!" one of the coaches shouted.

"So do I!" yelled the other.

"Gentlemen, gentlemen," the umpire said. "You're being subjective. One person's word is as good as another's." He smiled soothingly.

"Hold it," the home coach protested, pulling a rolled-up pamphlet from his back pocket. "Here's the rulebook. We've always gone by the rulebook."

The umpire stifled a snicker. "Oh, that old thing," he said. "Nobody believes in it anymore. It's a collection of misinformation."

"It is?" the coaches asked, surprised.

"Why, that book is chock-full of mistakes," the ump replied. "For one thing, it doesn't tell how baseballs are manufactured, which proves it's unscientific. It's been around since Abner Doubleday. Who knows how many errors have been added as it's been handed down?"

"Wow, I never thought of it that way before," the visiting coach said.

The home coach frowned. "But if the rulebook is no good, how can we come up with a way to play the game?"

The umpire smiled. "Why, democratically, of course. We'll have the fans vote every time we need a rule. Go along with the crowd, so to speak."

Shrugging, the coaches returned to their dugouts. "Play ball!" the new ump cried again.

The pitcher let fly another fastball, high and inside. When the batter failed to swing, the ump turned to the crowd. "Let's vote," he yelled. "How many think that was a strike?"

An affirmative roar went up from half the fans. The other half booed.

"And how many thought it was a ball?" the ump asked.

The second half screamed approval, while the first half growled.

"It was a strike, idiot!" a fan yelled.

"Any fool could see it was a ball!" shouted another.

Suddenly someone threw a popcorn box, and a fistfight broke out. Within seconds the stands were a surging mass of punching and kicking.

"I quit!" announced the pitcher, hurling his glove to the ground. "What's the use of pitching if nobody will call the strikes?"

"I quit, too," said the batter. "No point in hitting if foul and fair are the same thing." He flung his bat away in disgust, hitting the other team's pitcher.

"Ow!" the pitcher cried, and before long the dugouts were packed with players trying to strangle each other.

"Stop!" shouted the home coach over the din. "There's only one way to resolve this. We've got to get the old umpire back!"

There was a pause in the commotion as fans and players turned their ears to the coach. But then the coach frowned.

"On second thought," he worried, "the old ump would probably throw us all out of the stadium now, the way we're acting. So let's not."

"Yeah!" screamed the crowd and the players, resuming their battle.

The new umpire finished his plate dusting and looked up at the chaos raging around him. "Uh—play ball?" he said uncertainly.

Nobody was listening.

4

Whatever Is

*P*ure

PURE: (adjective) (1) being free from what weakens or pollutes; (2) free from moral fault or guilt; (3) marked by chastity. Synonyms: undiluted, innocent, stainless, clean, unsullied, chaste.

❧

Schopenhauer's Law

"If you put a spoonful of wine in a barrel full of sewage, you get sewage. If you put a spoonful of sewage in a barrel of wine, you get sewage."

❧

A Champion for Chastity*

by Amy Nappa and Jody Brolsma

To Esther Splaine, they are simply "her girls." But these eleven teenagers meet with Esther for more than "girl talk." They're members of Girls Against Premarital Sex, a support group for teens who want to remain abstinent until marriage. Once a week, Esther gathers her girls to discuss strategies for dealing with boyfriends who want to have sex. They engage in role-playing sessions to help them practice ways to say "No." They talk about the lines they've heard and the struggles they've had. Most of all, these young women realize that they're not alone in their pursuit of purity.

"I tell my girls to call me any time, twenty-four hours a day, if they need help. I've got five kids of my own. What's eleven more?" Esther smiles. She also requires that group members attend a church, temple, or mosque weekly or join a religious youth group. In a culture that generally accepts teen sexual activity, Esther is giving her girls the courage and confidence to stand up for virtue. Often it may seem like a losing battle. But to Esther, it's worth it.

"These girls have the same dreams other girls have—they dream of getting married, having babies, and living in a nice house. Sex before marriage has a way of taking all that away."

Esther is giving her girls more than an opportunity to fulfill their dreams. She's weaving a support system—a safety net—that girls can rely on when the pressure gets tough. She's giving them the skills and the voice to tell others that purity is important. And she's standing up for morality when other adults would rather turn away.

Often we're embarrassed or unsure how to handle the issue of purity. So we mumble a few awkward phrases or don't say anything at all. But if you don't say something, you can bet that someone else will. . .and it's likely that person won't share your values. Take a cue from Esther. Be open about sexual purity. Offer realistic solutions to tough situations. Encourage kids to get involved in church activities. Be a champion for chastity (you may be the only one your kids see). Make it clear that your kids can call on you twenty-four hours a day. Most importantly, give them a passion for purity.

Mother Teresa on Purity

God is purity Himself; nothing impure can come before Him, but I don't think God can hate, because God is love and God loves us in spite of our misery and sinfulness. He is our loving Father and so we have only to turn to Him. God cannot hate; God loves because He is love, but impurity is an obstacle to seeing God. This doesn't mean only the sin of impurity, but any attachment, anything that takes us away from God, anything that makes us less Christlike, any hatred, any uncharitableness is also impurity. If we are full of sin, God cannot fill us, because even God Himself cannot fill what is full. That's why we need forgiveness to become empty, and then God fills us with Himself.

In recent years, hundreds of thousands of American teenagers have responded to the call for sexual purity by making a promise to live according to the following pledge:

The True Love Waits Pledge

"Believing that true love waits, I make a commitment to God, myself, my family, my friends, my future mate, and my future children to be sexually abstinent from this day until the day I enter a biblical marriage relationship."

❧

Not long ago, we were able to interview Christian pop and Latin music star Jaci Velasquez. A young, single woman, she talked about the importance of sexual purity in her life. We're happy to share her thoughts with you here. . .

JACI VELASQUEZ ON PURITY

Mike Nappa: In your opinion, what's the biggest problem facing teenagers today?

Jaci Velasquez: In my heart there's one thing. It's the abstinence thing. I think that's one of the biggest problems right now.

Nappa: Teenagers take sex too casually?

Velasquez: Yeah! I think they take it way too casually. . .and I think that's one of the biggest problems right now. I know the drugs and the pressure, all those things, but to me it's the abstinence, they're not being true to that. That's one of the command-ments God put in the Bible.

Nappa: You wrote a song about that, right?

Velasquez: Yeah. "I Promise To" [from the album *Heavenly Place*]. It's about a promise to wait for my husband.

Nappa: What advice would you give other teenagers about purity?

Velasquez: I know there's a lot of programs going on. People are making a pledge to stay pure. I think that's the greatest thing going on right now. It goes back to not being a wimp, to being strong in your faith and your walk. To make that promise, to bring it in your own life. I know it sounds dumb to say, "Look at me, I'm a virgin and I'm cool." But it's not, because I'm not embarrassed about it.

I had this friend sleep over the other night. She has a boyfriend and they're really serious. She's fifteen and he's eighteen. She told me what had happened and why she wasn't a virgin anymore, and all I could tell her was, "I know you already messed up, but pray to the Lord. He can't give you back your virginity. He can't give you that back. But He can forgive you and say, 'I'll give you back the purity that you've lost.'" I don't know how to word that. Telling people that you are a virgin is a great way. It's a very private thing, but if you get to know somebody, that's the way to break through and let people know.

Nappa: Kind of an unashamed virginity?

Velasquez: Yeah! Not to be ashamed of what you are or who you are. That has to be the best way to help.

❧

ALL THAT GLITTERS

Imagine, if you will, that you've happened upon a jewelry case in one of those fancy mall stores. All around you are glittering gems and prettily adorned salespeople. But the case in front of you holds only four seemingly identical gold bands.

"Hmmm," you think to yourself as you move in for a closer look. Four gold bands. That's it. Your eye catches the price tag on the first ring. It reads "$100." Curious, you check the prices on the other three rings: the second one reads "$200"; the third is priced at "$300"; and the fourth—which, as best you can tell, looks identical to the first three—is a whopping "$400."

"Excuse me," you say to the nearest salesperson, "why is this last gold ring four hundred dollars, and all the others hundreds less?"

The salesclerk smiles and explains this way: "Gold is a rare metal, so rare that it's only found in 0.0000005 percent of the earth's crust—and even then it's most often mixed with other metals like copper and iron, and in igneous rocks like granite. So, before any of these rings can be made, they must first be separated from the other, impure elements. For instance, in some gold mines in the United States, three tons of rock must be removed to yield only one ounce of gold!

"This separation is done by first grinding a gold-bearing stone to dust, then using cyanide to separate gold, copper, silver, and other metals from the rock. Next, the metals are treated with zinc and acid to further separate the gold from the unwanted metals. Then the remaining solution—which still contains impurities like copper, iron, and zinc in it—is cast into a mold. From there it's further refined and measured."

The salesperson reaches in the case and pulls out the first gold band, which is priced at $100. "This ring is made up of twenty-four parts, called carats," the clerk says. "And in truth, less than half of this one is really gold—it's called ten carat gold because only 10/24ths of it is gold. The other 14/24ths of it are made up of some other metals like silver and copper." The clerk shrugs. "The lowest percentage of gold in this means the lowest price."

The clerk picks up the second and third rings. "This one is fourteen carat—or fourteen parts gold. A better mix, to be sure, but still just over half of it is gold. Thus, a little more expensive, but not too much more. This next ring is eighteen carat gold—or made of 75 percent gold. Still better, but not the best."

Finally the clerk picks up the four hundred dollar ring. "This," the salesperson says with admiration, "is twenty-four carat gold—all gold with no measurable impurities mixed into its makeup."

The clerk looks back at you and smiles. "And that's why it's the most expensive of all the rings here. Because it's pure gold."

You nod your thanks and walk away with one question still left in your mind, *If purity is so valued in metals like gold, I wonder why it's given so little value in people. . .*

And that's a question only you can answer.

❧

SPEAKING OF PURITY. . .

"The prince of this world [the devil], who knows whereof we are made, will not fail to improve the occasion to disturb, though he cannot pollute, the heart which God has cleansed from all unrighteousness."

JOHN WESLEY, as quoted in
John Wesley's Little Instruction Book

"There's nothin' like layin' on your belly 'n, stickin' your muzzle in a clean, runnin' stream!"
Cowboy proverb, as recorded by
KEN ALSTAD in *Savvy Sayin's*

"No greater mischief can happen to a Christian people than to have God's word taken from them, or falsified, so that they no longer have it pure and clear."

MARTIN LUTHER, as quoted in
Martin Luther's Little Instruction Book

*"My strength is as the strength of ten,
because my heart is pure."*
ALFRED LORD TENNYSON, as quoted on
Quoteworld.eilc.org

"The richest soil, uncultivated, produces the rankest weeds."

PLUTARCH, as quoted by
JOHN MAXWELL in
It's Just a Thought

"The example of great and pure individuals is the only thing that can lead us to noble thoughts and deeds."

ALBERT EINSTEIN, as quoted on
Quoteworld.eilc.org

*"Go West, young man
when the evil go East;
go West, young man,
find a heart that's golden."*
MICHAEL W. SMITH, in the song
"Go West, Young Man"
from the album of the same title

"The instrument through which you see God is your whole self. And if a man's self is not kept clean and bright, his glimpse of God will be blurred—like the Moon seen through a dirty telescope."

C. S. LEWIS in
Mere Christianity

*"You don't have to compromise
to be recognized."*
Clean comedian JONATHAN SLOCUMB,
as quoted in *Christian Single* magazine

"I promise to be true to You, to live my life in purity as unto You, waiting for the day when I hear You say, 'Here is the one I have created just for you.' "

JACI VELASQUEZ, in the song
"I Promise" from the album *Heavenly Place*

THE WORD ON PURITY. . .

*[Jesus said,] "Blessed are the pure in heart,
for they shall see God."*
MATTHEW 5:8 NASB

Since we have these promises, dear friends, let us purify ourselves from everything that contaminates body and spirit, perfecting holiness out of reverence for God.

2 CORINTHIANS 7:1 NIV

If you keep yourself pure, you will be a utensil God can use for his purpose. Your life will be clean, and you will be ready for the Master to use you for every good work.

2 Timothy 2:21 NLT

He [God] wants each of you to learn to control your own body in a way that is holy and honorable. Don't use your body for sexual sin like the people who do not know God.

1 Thessalonians 4:4–5 NCV

Marriage should be honored by all, and the marriage bed kept pure, for God will judge the adulterer and all the sexually immoral.

Hebrews 13:4 NIV

❧

PICTURES OF PURITY

In a world where we're bombarded daily with images of war, violence, filth, and evil, sometimes we need a visual reminder to help us focus our minds on purity. Here's a project that will help you do just that.

Begin by thinking about what images represent purity to you. The innocence of a newborn baby. The smile of a child. A bride wearing a trailing white gown. A field of flowers. Clean sheets drying in rays of sunshine. A mountain blanketed in undefiled snow.

Now take your camera and begin capturing these images on film. If you're not much of a photographer, gather a stack of magazines and begin looking for pictures such as those you've listed. When you have a collection, arrange them as a collage, then frame your creation. Hang this in your home or workplace where your eyes will fall upon it often. Every time you see these pictures, let your mind dwell on purity. It does exist.

❧

Purity before God is more than just sexual, it is a life lived—and gifts given—with a pure heart.

MARTIN'S GIFT

Martin had a problem.

Long after his wife and children had gone to bed, Martin was still wide awake. He stared out the window of his simply furnished living room, thinking. No doubt he sighed a time or two. Most likely he paced the worn floor as well. Finally he plopped down into his favorite chair.

Martin did not know what to do!

It was Christmas Eve, but he had no gifts for any of his six children. None. Zero. Zilch. Nothing.

Martin's work as a minister didn't pay enough to buy even one present for Christmas. Still, he desperately wanted to give something to his children, something to remind them of his love for them—and something to help them remember God's greatest gift to the world—His Son, Jesus.

Martin gazed deeply into the flame of the single candle that lit his room. He prayed silently for God's help.

Then, while his wife and children slept soundly in their rooms. . .

Martin began to grin.

Leaping from his chair, he bounded across the room.

Then he smiled again.

He found a fresh sheet of parchment and gathered his pen and ink.

He gave a short chuckle.

Then he sat back down by the candle and went to work, humming a little tune as he wrote. Hours later, deep into the night, he finally put down his pen. He sighed. He closed his eyes. And he dropped off to sleep, a merry look still on his face.

Next morning, like all Christmases with children, this best of all days started early—and with lots of noise! The children came bouncing out of bed, hopping, jumping, clattering, running, and giggling—into the living room where Martin slept.

Awakening with a cheery twinkle in his eyes, Martin gathered the family around him. Holding his youngest child in his lap, Martin declared he had a gift for all the children there. Then he sang these words to the world for the very first time:

"Away in a manger, no crib for his bed,

The little Lord Jesus laid down his sweet head;

The stars in the bright sky looked down where he lay,

The little Lord Jesus asleep on the hay. . ."

Martin Luther, pastor, theologian, reformer, and father, gave his children all he could—the gift of a song given out of a pure heart of love for his kids. It's been nearly five hundred years since Martin first sang those words as a holiday present for his children—but people of all ages still sing "Away in a Manger" today. And it is the gifts we give from pure hearts of love for others today that are the ones that will also last a lifetime—and beyond.

Why don't you give a gift like that this week?

Even our attempts to reach others with the gospel of Christ must be grounded in a purity of heart and actions that reveals both our true selves—and our one, true Savior.

*And so we're proud to close this chapter
with the reminder to pursue pureness of
motives in Jody Brolsma's delightful play. . .*

THE CONVERSION OF
A PREACHER MAN*

by Jody Wakefield Brolsma

PLOT SUMMARY

A visit from a heavenly messenger changes Trev's
idea of sharing one's faith.

CHARACTERS

Trev Rogers—He's a young math teacher with a
  Barney Fife-ish attitude about his
  Christianity.

Pastor—This person needs a good preaching
  voice.

Lynette—A history teacher.

Paul—An English teacher.

Angela—A young Spanish teacher.

Dan—The school janitor, he is a little older,
  gruff and grumpy.

Messenger—A female, similar in build and age
  to Angela, she is aggressive, with a sense of
  humor. (This part could be played by the
  same person who is Angela.)

Teachers—Two to four anonymous teachers act

as background extras in the teachers' lounge.

Setting

Most of the action takes place in the teachers' lounge at school, where there are tables, chairs, posters, a coffee pot, plastic cups, and stacks of papers. Trev's room need only consist of a bed (or something similar) and a nightstand with an alarm clock on it. His bedroom can be set to the far side of the stage left.

Props

A Bible, Christian tracts (from a distance, any brochure will do), book bags or briefcases, books, a radio with headphones, a white baseball cap with a large cross drawn or pinned to the front, a tie, a broom, garbage cans with plastic liners, and taped organ music. You'll also need appropriate stage lights and sound.

The Script
"The Conversion of a Preacher Man"

(Stage is dark except for spotlight on Trev, who is sitting in a chair in the teachers' lounge area and holding his Bible. He's dressed for work in a shirt and tie; looking up, as if listening to someone. From offstage, Pastor's voice begins.)

Pastor: And that's why Jesus says, "You are the

light of the world." We need to shine out God's light in everything we do, in everything we say, in everything we are, each and every day. Jesus didn't say, "You are the light of the world. . .sometimes" or "You are the light of the world when you feel like it." He said, "You are the light of the world." Period. (Pauses.) As we close with the final verse of "O the Deep, Deep Love of Jesus," ask yourself, "Am I shining out God's light in everything I do? Am I being a light to *my* world?"

(Organ music plays softly.)

Trev: (Prays looking up, as if talking to God.) *Dear God, help me to be a light to the people in my world. . .even though I'm not sure how. I mean, God, I'm not exactly "light" material. You see me mess up all the time.* (Smiles.) *But You still love me. I guess that's what I want people to know—that You love them no matter what. But as far as this "being-a-light" thing. . .I'm not sure how. I try to show people that I'm Christian, but. . .*

(Lights go up and teachers rush into lounge, laughing, talking, and joking around. Some are grabbing papers and rushing out; others are sitting down with cups of coffee. A bell rings and the lounge clears except for Trev, Lynette, Paul, and a few other teachers, who are grading papers, reading, or chatting quietly. Trev greets a few teachers, then bumps into Lynette.)

Trev: Lynette, I heard that your guest speaker last Friday was great! Kids came into class raving about Mrs. Merriam's Civil War general.

Lynette: He was great all right, until he told the class that soldiers in the Civil War dropped out of school to join the army. I had three seniors get up to enlist!

Trev: (Laughing) Seniors will do anything to get out of school! Hey, how was your weekend? I heard that your parents were going to be in town.

Lynette: Yeah, it was good to see them again. I really miss them, and it's so expensive to fly out there. Sometimes I wish that Tyler and Katie could see more of their grandparents, but it's just been hard lately.

Trev: Yeah, I know how that can be. I really miss my parents, too. (Reaches for a baseball cap, which he keeps in his back pocket or tucked into his waistband.) What with them being born-again-Christian missionaries in Africa spreading the Good News about Jesus to all the primitive tribes there, starting new churches, translating the Bible

into native languages, and leading four
Bible studies, they don't get home much. I
just remember to "kneel in my prayer-closet
and lift their souls to God" for a few hours
each night. That makes them seem closer.

Lynette: (Rolls eyes and gets up.) That's a. . .
uh. . .great idea, Trev. I'll remember it. I
need to make a phone call. (Exits quickly.)

(Trev takes off cap and goes to the coffee pot
for a refill. Paul is leaning against the wall reading
a book.)

Trev: Hi, Paul. How's it going?

Paul: (Looks up from book.) Good, as far as
Mondays go.

Trev: Some good reading there?

Paul: Yeah, it's Matthew Crider's newest book.
I've been trying to finish it for weeks, but
it's tough to find the time. You should read
it, it's incredible.

Trev: I'd love to, but (putting cap back on) I
spend most of my reading time digging
into God's Word. My day just isn't complete unless I've drunk the sweet milk of
Scripture for a few hours. But for lighter
reading, I've found that these "Tracts of
Truth" are excellent, too. (Pulls out tracts.)
Why don't you take one and let me know
what you think.

Paul: (Moving to a chair, focusing on the book) I'm pretty busy with this book. But thanks anyway. (Turns attention to book.)

Trev: Okay, well, praise the Lord!

(Trev removes his cap and takes his coffee to the table, where he sits down to grade some papers. After a few seconds, Angela enters with a book.)

Trev: Oh, hi, Angela. How's life in freshman Spanish?

Angela: Bueno, bueno! Today's extra credit day, so the kids are bringing in Mexican food. I'm stuffed! I think next year I'll have them write stories in Spanish—it'd be less fattening!

(Both laugh.)

Angela: Hey, speaking of food, we missed you at the faculty dessert last week. Where were you?

(Other teachers in the room groan.)

Trev: (Puts on cap.) Oh, I was strengthening my spirit at the tenth Annual Born-Again-Christian Revival and Renewal Meeting. Didn't you get a flier? I put them in everyone's box last Monday.

Angela: Uh. . .no. . .I guess not.

Trev: Well, that okay, because I go to three
"Diggin'-Deep-in-the-Word" Bible studies
each week. You can come to one of those
instead. We're studying spiritual gifts in
one, the fruit of the Spirit in another, and
the book of Hebrews in the third. Sounds
fascinating, right?

Angela: I–I'm not sure.

Trev: If you don't have a Bible, I can loan you
one. I've got three of each version.

Angela: It's not that. It's just that I'm really
busy at home these days. Things have been
tight, so I'm doing some bookkeeping for
my brother's company in the evenings. I
miss the time with my kids, but it's helping
make ends meet. So Bible study is pretty
much out.

Trev: I see. (Starts to remove hat, changes
mind.) How about reading one of these
"Tracts of Truth" instead? They're really
short—it'll hardly take any time at all!
Here's one I think you'll really enjoy.

Angela: Well, okay. I can't promise you that I'll
have the time to read it or anything. But,
thanks just the same.

Trev: No problem. And remember, praise the
Lord!

(Everyone freezes in the teachers' lounge. Lights fade on lounge, then go up on Trev's bedroom. Trev enters, sets down briefcase, and throws cap on the bed. He takes off his shirt and tie, revealing a white T-shirt underneath. He sits on the bed and takes off his shoes, then puts on a baggy pajama shirt over his T-shirt.)

Trev: What a day! Christianity is tiring, God! There are so many people who need You. I mean, like Angela. She's alone in the city, raising two kids on her own, struggling financially, and just seems so lonely. If only I could show her that knowing You helps fill in all those gaps, that walking with You makes life. . .different. I try, Lord, honestly, but for some reason, nobody ever wants to listen. Maybe if I practice. . . (Picks up cap, tucks it in waistband, and stands in front of imaginary mirror. Practices putting it on, as if in a quick-draw shootout. Talks confidently to mirror.) Hi, I'm a born-again-know-where-I've-been-now-headed-to-heaven-Christian. ("Draws" his cap again.) Do you know Jesus? He knows you! (Draws his cap once more.) I want you to know I've spent hours kneeling in my prayer-closet lifting up your very soul to God. (Leaves the cap on; quick-draws a tract.) May I share about God with you?

Praise the Lord! (Takes off cap and tosses it on the bed.) Aw, I don't know. Something's just not right. How can I make people see, God?

(Discouraged, Trev crawls into bed. Lights dim. After a few seconds, the Messenger enters. She's wearing a white mask that covers her eyes and nose, baggy white sweats, a white baseball cap, and high-top sneakers. She wears a whistle around her neck, which she blows loudly. Trev jumps.)

Trev: Wha. . .?
Messenger: Trev Rogers, right?
Trev: Yeah, but who're. . .what're you. . .how'd . . .what's going on?
Messenger: Take it easy, Trev. You and I just need to have a little chat. Your Father asked me to come down and help you out. Explain a few new ground rules, go over. . .
Trev: (Interrupting) Dad? How do you know my dad? Did he give you a key to get in here? Help me with what? Who are you?
Messenger: Of course I know your dad! A wonderful man, but not the topic of our little tête-à-tête. I'm referring to your *Father* (pointing upward) you know, your *heavenly* Father.
Trev: You mean. . .(Looks up, then looks at Messenger.)

Messenger: (Nodding) The one and only!

Trev: Then that would make you a—that means you're an. . .

Messenger: Yep. And a very busy one, so let's get down to business.

Trev: But wait, shouldn't you have wings or something? And what about your halo?

Messenger: The wing thing was scratched years ago. They kept getting tangled up in telephone lines. Same with the halos. (Pointing to baseball cap.) These are much more comfy—wash-and-wear—a lifesaver in case of a bad-hair day. . . (Looking up suddenly) Oh, sorry, back to business.

Trev: Just a minute. (Reaches for his cap, which is lying on the floor.)

Messenger: (Grabs it before he can.) Uh, uh, uh (shaking head). That's just what I'm here to talk about.

Trev: But I'm trying! I'll get faster, I promise. I've always been slower than everyone else. Even back in third grade in Mrs. Reinebach's class, when everyone else was learning their multiplication tables, I was still—

Messenger: Brushing up on your subtraction. Yes, I know. But that's not what I'm here about. (Holding up cap) Trev, this isn't what shows people that you're a child of God. (Picking up tracts from nightstand)

Neither do these! And especially not your long-winded speeches about what an amazing Christian you are.

Trev: But I'm supposed to be a light, shining out God's love.

Messenger: Yes, but you're not supposed to *blind* people!

Trev: So what am I supposed to do?

Messenger: Well, first of all, get rid of these things. (Tosses cap and tracts offstage.) Whew, I feel worlds better already, don't you?

Trev: (Looking longingly offstage) Well, actually. . .

Messenger: Now stand up straight.

(Trev stands at attention.)

Messenger: Look me in the eyes. Do you feel like a child of God?

Trev: (Relaxes, looking down.) In my pajamas?

Messenger: In your pajamas, in a clown suit, in a dress. . .who cares?

Trev: Well, I'd feel pretty ridiculous in a dress. . . .

Messenger: Trev! Listen to me! Your faith lives in here (touching Trev's chest), not out here (picking up the tie from where Trev dropped it).

Trev: (Discouraged) Aw, I knew I'd get it all wrong. I'm a flop at being a Christian. Why can't I be like those guys at church who always have it together? They're never late for service; they teach Sunday school, lead Bible studies, support missionaries, and tell all their coworkers about Christ. . .

Messenger: And that's why two of those guys are next on my list for a visit this evening. They've got their own problems, too.

Trev: (Mouth drops.) No!

Messenger: Yes! Now would you listen up? Time's a-wastin', and I have an idea that those two visits are going to be even tougher. (Under her breath) What a night!

Trev: You've got to be kidding! If *those* guys have problems, I'm really messed up.

Messenger: (Sighing) Trev, Trev, Trev. We're going to try something different. (Turns him toward bed.) Crawl back into bed and go to sleep.

Trev: (Getting under covers) I'm such an awful Christian that you're giving up on me?

Messenger: No, you're not an awful Christian. You love God and really want others to know Him, too. Your heart is perfect! So, that's what I'm going to leave you with tomorrow: no tracts, no Bible, no long speeches, no missionary letters. Just your heart.

Trev: (Yawns.) Just. . .my heart?

Messenger: (Chuckling to herself as Trev falls asleep) The cold-turkey method. It's a toughie, but it works every time. Poor guy won't know what hit him in the morning. (Checking watch) And now for the real challenge—two ultra-super Christians with faith as thin as a choir robe. (Looking to heaven) You love giving me these, don't You? (Walking offstage) Yeah, yeah, I know.

(Stage lights dim for a few seconds, then brighten. Trev's alarm goes off—an egg timer will work for a sound effect. Trev turns the alarm off, sits up, yawns, and stretches.)

Trev: What a night! I had the weirdest dream—an angel in a sweat suit came and told me I had to teach multiplication to some people at church. (Confused look) Or something like that. Oh well. Better get ready for work. (Reaches for cap on nightstand but can't find it.) Where in the world. . . ? (Looks around room.) Hmmm, maybe I put it with my tracts. (Opens nightstand drawer, but it's empty. Begins searching frantically.) They're gone! Someone stole all of my tracts! (Stops and thinks.) But then they'd read them and might become Christians, which would actually be a good thing. (Frantic again) But what am I supposed to do? My missionary letters were with them, too, so I can't even show those off. Wait! Where's my Bible? I mean, really!

You just can't trust. . . (Stops. Sits on the bed.) The angel. I remember the angel. In my dream, the angel took all my. . . Then that means my dream. . .wasn't a dream.

(Lights go out on Trev's room. Lights go up on teachers' lounge. A few teachers are bustling around, getting papers, grabbing a quick cup of coffee to take to class, or stapling papers together. Paul enters, sits down, and begins grading a stack of papers. The bell rings, and all but a few teachers clear out. Lynette enters carrying a radio with headphones.)

Lynette: Assigned too much homework, I see.

Paul: (Shaking head) I remember when I thought being a teacher would be easy—no homework. These English essays take forever to grade!

Lynette: Why the rush to get them graded? This is your break period.

Paul: I'm going to my little brother's bachelor party tonight. I'd hate to be grading an English essay when they bring out Lola, the Belly-Dancing Legend.

Lynette: Stop! I don't want to hear any more about what goes on at a bachelor party! My husband had one, and it's probably better that I remain in the dark.

Paul: (Laughing) okay. Anyway, tonight's out, and tomorrow I'm sure I'll have a headache the size of Mount Rushmore from all the. . .

(Trev enters, looking a little out of it. Paul stops talking and goes back to his papers. Lynette starts to put her headphones on but stops when she notices how odd Trev looks.)

Lynette: Trev? Are you okay?
Trev: Yeah. (Reaches for his back pocket but then remembers. Smiles nervously.) Fine.
Lynette: You look. . .different. I mean, it's a good kind of different but definitely. . . different. Did you get a haircut or something?
Trev: No, it's just that. . .well, it must be that I was up all night praising the L. . . (Trev is overcome by a coughing fit, cutting off his sentence. When he recovers, he continues.) As I was saying, I was up all night. . . (short cough) pr–practicing my tuba. (Intended to say "praising the Lord" but the words came out wrong. With a quizzical look, he mouths "practicing my tuba" to the audience.)
Lynette: (Slowly) Practicing your. . .tuba? Why? I mean, I didn't even know you played the tuba.
Trev: Um, well, it's something I've just recently —really—recently—taken up.
Lynette: Great, well, maybe if you keep

practicing hard you'll be able to play something at the faculty Christmas party.

Paul: Christmas party? Trev, I don't think you've
been to a faculty Christmas party in three
years.

Trev: Yeah (thinking aloud), not since I became
a born-again-know-where-I've-been. . .
(coughing fit again). Whew! Excuse me. I
meant to say, not since I became a Chri—
(short cough) Chr–chrysanthemum.
(Meant to say Christian, realizes what he
said and tries to recover.) Uh. . .freak! A
chrysanthemum freak! (Beginning to sweat
a bit) I spend all of my time cultivating my
garden and growing. . .chrysanthemums.

(Paul and Lynette look at each other oddly.)

Paul: I'd think you could take a night off to go
to a party.

Lynette: You could even bring some of your
flowers for decoration.

Trev: Sure, I. . .uh. . .guess I'd never thought of
that. (Changing the topic) Say, has anyone
seen Angela today? I gave her a tr. . .I gave
her something to read, and I wanted to talk
to her about it.

Paul: You haven't heard?

Trev: Heard what?

Lynette: She transferred to North Central

High. I guess it's closer to her house and her kids' school.

Paul: She'd been wanting to transfer for a while, but there wasn't an opening for a Spanish teacher. George Beardsley said that North Central called yesterday and asked for her after their Spanish teacher quit. It's kind of a tough area. She's got her work cut out for her.

Trev: (In his most holy-sounding voice) Well, then, I'd better kneel in my closet and pr. . . (short cough) pr–prune for her. (Covering his mistake) Uh. . .I mean. . .prune my chrysanthemums. (Pauses.) So I can take her some flowers. To encourage her.

Lynette: Trev, that's so thoughtful. I know that would mean a lot to Angela. She'll need all the encouragement she can get.

Paul: (Standing up) Look, you two, you're not helping me get this work done. I'll be in the library. (Starts to leave, then turns around.) And Trev, good luck on the tuba practice. (Exits.)

Lynette: Well, if you don't mind, I'm going to relax with Bach for the remainder of this all-too-short break. (Puts on headphones and relaxes in a chair or on the couch.)

Trev: (To himself) Great. I've succeeded in making a complete idiot of myself. Plus I'm expected to bring chrysanthemums to every occasion and play "Frosty the Snowman" on the tuba. (Pauses.) But, it was kind of nice to have people talk to me. . .almost as if they like me.

(Dan enters and changes the liners in the trash cans, then sweeps the floor.)

Dan: How's the preacher man today?
Trev: (Wryly) Not preaching today, I'm afraid.
Dan: (Sarcastically) Well, praise the Lord.
Trev: (Smiling) Great to have you back, Dan, I missed your words of encouragement last week.
Dan: Humph!
Trev: So how was your vacation?
Dan: (Doesn't look up.) Dandy.
Trev: What'd you see? Where'd you go?
Dan: Went to Florida. Saw my folks.
Trev: Sounds. . .great. (Starts to say something but decides against it. Opens a briefcase and gets out a stack of papers. There should be a few seconds of silence.)
Dan: (Still sweeping) My dad. . .died.

(Trev reaches for his hat, out of habit, but stops and runs his fingers through his hair. Pauses.)

Trev: (Slowly) I'm sorry. You must feel. . .sad.

Dan: He was a good man. (Looks up from sweeping.) A real good man. Gonna miss him.

Trev: (Softly) I know.

Dan: (Takes a deep breath.) Well, looks like I'm done in here. Got a stopped-up toilet in the boys' locker room. Someone tried to flush a freshman. (Starts to leave.)

Trev: Dan?

(Dan stops, turns around, Trev looks toward heaven, then at Dan.)

Trev: I'll be. . .I'll be praying for you.

Dan: (Pauses, then nods.) Sure. (Exits.)

(Lights go out except for a spotlight on Angela, now dressed in the Messenger's outfit.)

Angela: (Speaking to God) Yeah, You're right. He's gonna be okay. Just got caught up a bit much in the Christian-cliché thing. (Takes off mask.) Now for this North Central High assignment; we need to talk! There's this guy—yes, I know You know him—and he's got this problem. . .

(Walks offstage talking. Lights go out.)

5

Whatever Is

*L*ovely

LOVELY: (adjective) delightful for beauty, harmony, or grace. Synonyms: attractive, beautiful, handsome, alluring, exquisite, graceful, entrancing, lovesome.

❧

THE FACE OF BEAUTY*

by Alda Ellis

I was standing just inside the door of my local department store, picking up loose coins that had tumbled out, when my change purse fell open. To make matters worse, I was trying to protect myself from rain with a contrary umbrella that had definite thoughts of its own. Now that I was indoors, the umbrella naturally refused to close. Wondering if anyone would assist me, I was surprised to see help arrive from some unfamiliar faces. Several kind ladies actually stooped down next to me to help me quickly gather my coins. In the midst of confusion, I was a bit surprised that a frail, silver-haired lady stopped, bent down to help, and offered words of gentle humor while a young, bluejean-clad girl only darted a brief glance at me as she quickly passed by.

Now warm and dry inside the store, I strolled the aisles of the perfume department. I noticed the tremendously sophisticated marketing of products that were supposedly guaranteed to drastically improve every woman's appearance. Instantaneously absorbed in the promotions, posters, and campaigns of tote bags brimming with pretty tissue papers and attractive products, I almost forgot what I had come to buy. "Beauty's in a bottle and youth's in a jar," the captivating displays seemed to announce, but after my encounter with the elderly lady who helped me pick up my coins, I believe I had seen the true face of beauty.

Maybe you also have had the experience of seeing someone who you thought was quite beautiful from a distance or on the surface. Then you saw that same person react to a situation in a way that completely changed your initial impression of her, as well as your previous admiration of her beauty. Disagreeable tempers and unfriendly faces have no beauty about them. But a kind smile and an encouraging glance instantly transform an ordinary face into one of exquisite comeliness.

When I was in the third grade, I thought my teacher was extraordinarily pretty. She was the kindest, most patient woman who once discreetly gave the red-headed, freckle-faced boy who sat in the seat behind me a brand-new pair of jeans. She knew that he had been wearing the same pair for weeks. It was a loving gesture to a young boy whose father had left the family and whose hard-working mother struggled to simply put food on the table. Our teacher knew how innocently uncaring we third graders could be with our simplistic honesty, and so she remedied the potential problem in her own quiet and unassuming way.

Only years later, as I flipped through the timeworn pages of my grade school photo album, did I see how plain my teacher really looked. In the picture I have of our class, I notice first that she had a gentle smile. Her hair was pulled neatly back, and a painter's collar blouse framed her face. Although she appeared simple, her heart was anything but. She had taught us not only arithmetic, spelling, and handwriting, but also kindness, compassion, wisdom, and grace. Through my adoring third grade eyes, I had seen her as she really was—beautiful, simply beautiful—for I saw her with my heart.

True inward and outward beauty should be almost impossible to distinguish between, as one echoes the other. Cheeks glowing with a blush of peaches may only whisper of a woman's tender inner spirit. Never mind a milky, porcelain complexion, shiny chestnut tresses, or a smile that could stir music in the soul, for it is only with the heart that we can see what is invisible to the eye. True beauty is not merely skin deep; it originates clear down in the depths of the soul.

One of the hardest things to do is look beyond our own mirror and assess the true attributes of beauty as, through the ages, they have stood the test of time. The most beautiful of faces may now be adorned with wrinkles, but the eyes radiate a warmth and a smile that breaks forth like the morning light. Some good advice to heed is to live your life without concentrating on your age. You can become more beautiful as you grow older.

The most beautiful of all women seem to have in common some timeless qualities of beauty—grace, wisdom, thoughtfulness, kindness, compassion—and they carry them with a certain sense of confidence. These are the qualities of what I believe to be true beauty. They are accessible to every woman. We need only put them on and live our lives sheathed in their presence.

SEEN AND HEARD

I saw beauty today.
It laughed at me
From the mouth of an upside-down child
Hanging on the jungle gym at the park.

I tasted beauty today.
It was chocolate (of course)
And slid down my throat with the greatest
    of ease
Because my wife gave it as a gift for
    my birthday.

I felt beauty today.
It touched me when I closed my eyes
And turned my face toward the sun
And felt its warmth cover my skin like
    a blanket.

I heard beauty today.
It sang to me of Christ
Through the lips of a ten-year-old boy,
Nervous, but determined, during an
    elementary school Christmas play.

I smelled beauty today
On the neck of the woman who intertwines
    her life with mine.
It was not perfume, but something much
    better.
It was simply her presence, and the fragrance
    of love.

❧

SOMETIMES A LITTLY UGLY WORK CAN MAKE A BEAUTIFUL THING

Mike felt the paint stinging his eyes once more and strangled a curse in his throat. It would not do to utter profanity in this place. Still, he closed his eyes in frustration and let the tears flow out, washing away the burning sensation in his eyes.

He tried to sit up, remembering too late the ceiling only inches above and giving himself a knock on the head. A sigh escaped his lips as he collapsed backward on the scaffolding. "I'm a sculptor, not a painter!" he muttered for the hundredth time.

Four years. Four long years Michelangelo Buonarroti had been working on this blasted ceiling. Four years of his life, gone, with only these pictures on plaster to show for it.

He remembered ruefully the day when Pope Julius II had called him to Rome, saying he wanted sculptures to fill his courtyards. Now that was something Michelangelo could do! He'd spent months searching for just the right pieces of marble, envisioning the sculptures inside them, excited to bring life and beauty out of those heavy marble blocks. But when he returned with his marble, the Pope had changed his mind.

"I want you to paint it," Pope Julius II had said after leading the sculptor into the bare—and vast—Sistine Chapel. He pointed to the blank ceiling overhead and said simply, "I want it decorated."

Michelangelo was stunned. "But I am a sculptor!" he said. "I'm no painter. Get Raphael to do it. He is skillful with the brush."

"Nonsense," said the Pope. "Raphael is busy." And the decision had been made. Michelangelo the sculptor was now a painter, and his canvas would be the ten thousand-square-foot ceiling of the Sistine Chapel.

So began the thankless, unwanted task that Michelangelo now found himself performing. At first he tried hiring other artists to help with the job, but they couldn't match the skill of the sculptor. Before long he had sent them away, erasing what they'd done and re-doing the visions himself.

Month after month, each day was the same. Michelangelo worked alone, silently, lying back on a scaffold and painting the ceiling over his head. The paint dripped in his eyes, his arms and back and legs and neck ached from being cramped on the scaffolding day in and day out. The immensity of the task consumed him. He would start his days at first light, painting until the darkness of night filled his gloom. He often forgot to eat, couldn't bring himself to stop for sleep, even became ill from exhaustion. It was a hard job; a dirty job he had not wanted—but now one he was determined to finish.

Time and time again, Pope Julius II would climb the scaffold and ask, "When will you make an end?"

And time after time, Michelangelo would stretch his aching muscles, refocus on his plaster canvas, and say, "When I am done."

At long last, Michelangelo Buonarroti painted one last stroke on a corner of the ceiling, then let his brush drop to his side. At long last, the aching, filthy, lonely painter had finally finished his masterpiece.

Soon after, the scaffolding was taken down, the floors wiped clean, and the doors of the Sistine Chapel were flung open. Hundreds came to see Michelangelo's work, then thousands, then tens of thousands. And each gaze up onto the ceiling of the chapel revealed the same sights: Over three hundred figures—men, women, God, angels, and more—stretched across the vast expanse of Michelangelo's ten thousand-square-foot canvas. And each scene showed in beautiful detail the stories of Scripture—Creation, the fall of humanity, the great flood, and other timeless moments in the history of humankind.

Staring out of the center of this masterpiece was the hand of God reaching, longing, for the hand of the first man, Adam. From the tip of Michelangelo's paintbrushes had flowed the beauty of God and His creation. No artist had ever before, or has ever since, captured with such clarity that kind of eternal loveliness.

It is said that the great painter, Raphael—the same Raphael that Michelangelo had begged the Pope choose for the job—came himself to view the Sistine Chapel. He was so moved by what he saw that, upon leaving, he paused to thank God for being born in the same century as Michelangelo Buonarroti.

Painting the Sistine Chapel certainly was a dirty job, but imagine how much poorer our world would be if Michelangelo had not done it. Through his ugly years of toil and labor, we now have a timeless work of beauty that has enchanted millions of people for nearly five centuries—and counting.

A LOVELY LANGUAGE
FOR ALL WHO SEE

Many people (especially women) consider flowers one of the most lovely of God's creations. Why else would we spend so much time and money on gardens (along with the tools, seeds, fertilizer, and so on)? Flowers say "congratulations," "I'm sorry," "I love you," and more. Over time, specific flowers have actually come to represent different emotions and qualities. Here's a list of what a few popular flowers are considered to symbolize:

- Red chrysanthemum: Love
- White chrysanthemum: Truth
- Clematis: Mental beauty
- Daffodil: Regard
- White daisy: Innocence
- Gladiolus: Strength of character
- Marigold: Grief or despair
- Rose: Love
- Yellow tulip: Hopeless love
- Blue violet: Faithfulness
- Water lily: Purity of heart
- Zinnia: Thoughts of absent friends

Why not head to the florist and put together a lovely bouquet for a friend, sharing a message through the flowers? Be sure to intertwine a few strands of ivy throughout the blooms—it represents friendship.

❧

Recipe for a Lovely Day

STIR TOGETHER:
> One bucketful of sunshine
> A melody in your heart
> Three cups of fresh air
> A hint of a warm breeze

SPRINKLE IN:
> Two smiles
> One hug
> Three tablespoons of God's Word
> An ounce of prayer

Let simmer in a heart full of joy, then serve with generous scoops of laughter.

❧

Speaking of Loveliness. . .

*"If one desires to be loved,
one must also endeavor to be lovely."*
ANONYMOUS

"A kiss is a lovely trick designed by nature to stop speech when words become superfluous."

INGRID BERGMAN, as quoted on
Quoteworld.eilc.org

*"The most effective kind
of education is that a child should play
amongst lovely things."*
PLATO, as quoted in
Cole's Quotables on
Starlingtech.com

"Never lose an opportunity of seeing anything beautiful. Beauty is God's handwriting."

CHARLES KINGSLEY, as quoted by
WILLIAM R. EVANS III and
ANDREW FROTHINGHAM in *Crisp Toasts*

"If someone loves a flower, of which just one single blossom grows in all the millions and millions of stars, it is enough to make him happy just to look at the stars. He can say to himself, 'Somewhere, my flower is there. . .'"

THE LITTLE PRINCE, as quoted by
ANTOINE DE SAINT-EXUPÉRAY in
The Little Prince

*"The most beautiful thing
we can experience is the mysterious.
It is the source of all true art and science."*
ALBERT EINSTEIN,
as quoted on Starlingtech.com

"Beauty is a form of genius—is higher indeed than genius, as it needs no explanation. It is of the great facts in the world like sunlight, or spring-time, or the reflection in dark water of that silver shell we call the moon."

> OSCAR WILDE, as quoted in
> *Cole's Quotables* on Starlingtech.com

"I never thought through love we'd be making one as lovely as she, but isn't she lovely, made from love!"

> STEVIE WONDER, singing about his newborn daughter in the song "Isn't She Lovely" from the album *Songs in the Key of Life*

"Love came down at Christmas; Love all lovely, love divine; Love was born at Christmas, stars and angels gave the sign."

> CHRISTINA GEORGINA ROSSETTI,
> as quoted on Quoteworld.eilc.org

"A man should hear a little music, read a little poetry, and cultivate good thoughts every day of his life, in order that worldly cares may not obliterate the sense of the beautiful which God has planted in the human soul."

> GOETHE, as quoted by
> ALFRED MONTAPERT in
> *Words of Wisdom to Live By*

❧

THE WORD ON LOVELINESS. . .

How lovely on the mountains are the feet of him who brings good news, who announces peace and brings good news of happiness, who announces salvation, and says to Zion, "Your God reigns!"

ISAIAH 52:7 NASB

Be happy with the wife you married when you were young. She gives you joy, as your fountain gives you water. She is as lovely and graceful as a deer. Let her love always make you happy; let her love always hold you captive.

PROVERBS 5:18–19 NCV

The right word spoken
at the right time is
as beautiful as gold apples
in a silver bowl.
PROVERBS 25:11 NCV

Don't be concerned about the outward beauty that depends on fancy hairstyles, expensive jewelry, or beautiful clothes. You should be known for the beauty that comes from within, the unfading beauty of a gentle and quiet spirit, which is so precious to God. That is the way the holy women of old made themselves beautiful.

1 PETER 3:3–5 NLT

How lovely is your dwelling place, O LORD Almighty! My soul yearns, even faints, for the courts of the LORD; my heart and my flesh cry out for the living God. PSALM 84:1–2 NIV

For our money, few things in life are lovelier than the unique relationship a parent has with his or her children. After you read the following story from Dennis Swanberg, we're sure you'll agree.

HOW ABOUT THOSE COWBOYS?*

by Dennis Swanberg

A lot of people have asked the question: "How do I say 'I love you'?" Florists want you to say it with flowers. Jewelers want you to say it with diamonds.

Elizabeth Barrett Browning asked, "How do I love thee? Let me count the ways." For years Elizabeth Barrett had been an invalid, bedfast in her room. The first time Robert Browning came to visit her, she sat up. The second time he visited, she walked around the room. The third time, they eloped. How's that for the power of love?

My oldest son, Chad, took adolescence by storm! By the time we moved from the pastorate at First Baptist Church of West Monroe,

Louisiana, to Southwestern Baptist Theological Seminary where I became the special assistant to the president in seminary relations, Chad was full-bloom into puberty. (No, that's not a style of music—although Chad was just the "B-natural" chord. The vibrations were taking years off my life.) Nevertheless, Chad and I continued to bond as father and son as we shared our points of view with each other.

I remember when Chad decided I was using the phrase "I love you" too often in public. It especially bothered him when I said it around his buddies, creatures of his same kind. It seemed as though mutation was manifesting itself before my very eyes.

Sadly enough, one night Chad said, "Dad, we need to find a code phrase to say 'I love you' instead of actually saying it." I listened quietly as he explained that we could have a phrase like the father and son on the television sitcom *Home Improvement.* He told me the dad would say, "How about those [Detroit] Tigers?" as an incognito way of saying "I love you."

I couldn't believe this was happening to the Swan. I have always verbalized my love to my boys. Many men have trouble saying "I love you," and I really believe our children need to hear these words often. But Chad had heard them often enough. He wanted me to be more like other dads.

So "preacher" dad backed off and said, "Okay, what should our code be?"

Chad suggested, "How about those Cowboys?"

I conceded. That night [when] I tucked him —excuse me—said good night to him, I simply said, "Sleep well, son, and, uh, 'How about those Cowboys?' "

Chad gave me a high-five, and that was that.

I walked down the hall, fell into my big blue chair, and muttered, "How about those Cowboys?" I didn't feel like I had made a first down. Instead, I felt like I had gotten a fifteen-yard penalty for being a dad on the cutting edge. My offensive strategy was out of sync, and the game plan was going to a preventive defense rather than an aggressive attack on the gridiron of fatherhood. I would have to wait for that hug and "I love you." I was a bit jealous of Lauree. She still had a full-fledged and dominating offense. She still received the hugs and "I love yous" of her older teenaged son.

I longed for expressions of love with my boys. I knew, however, that I needed to understand Chad's language of love. I had to learn to be bilingual with a son going through the change of adolescence.

Then George Strait came to Shreveport, Louisiana, to give a concert; I'll never be the same. He may not know it, but I believe God brought him to our state.

When Lauree found out about the concert in Shreveport, she immediately bought tickets for our entire family. Lauree loves George Strait. So do Chad and Dusty. And I must confess, I like him, too. We are a country-western music family. But the concert was an hour-and-a-half drive from West Monroe, and it was on a Saturday evening. I usually try to rest and polish my sermon on the night before the Lord's Day, but that Saturday night we dressed in Western apparel and prepared to go to the concert.

Lauree pulled out all the stops with her outfit. I never knew a preacher's wife could be so good looking! Lauree was the Barbara Mandrell of ministers' wives. The Swan was decked out, too. I was the Garth Brooks of Baptists. I had on my ostrich boots, and my belt had a shiny new buckle with a huge *S* on it.

I wanted to leave early enough to get some seafood in Shreveport and still have time to choose a good seat for the concert. I said, "Let's get going. Let's crank it on out. Come on, Mama, you can redo your lipstick in the car."

We finally pulled into the parking lot and still had a half-mile walk to the coliseum. I took off, leading the pack, walking several steps ahead of the family. Lauree called to me, and I looked back but didn't see Chad. He was behind the Suburban. He had just lost his deluxe shrimp dinner. Evidently the excitement was too much for him.

Lauree mouthed to me not to say a word.

Oh, he'll be all right, I thought. *I'll get him some popcorn, a hot dog, and nachos. He'll be as good as new.*

When we entered the coliseum, it was packed with every country-western music lover from the regions of Texas, Arkansas, and North Louisiana. Looking at how everyone was dressed, one would have thought that the best-dressed cowboy and cowgirl would win a backstage pass to hang out with George.

Down the hallway was a cardboard cutout of George Strait. We took our camera out of its holster and persuaded a Dolly Parton look-alike to take our picture with George. I love that picture. We were having fun. It was the first time our entire family looked like we were not in the ministry. I felt like a tenured usher on a mission to stardom in country music.

Lauree was singing along to "Amarillo by Morning," and I found myself thinking, *Will they call it preaching when I deliver the sermon tomorrow morning?*

While Chad and Dusty began harmonizing to "All My Exes Live in Texas," I started looking for the nearest exit. I was thinking about how to get out of there quick enough to beat the traffic for the long drive home. I finally got into the concert when George started singing about the Heartland. I stopped worrying and started laughing, singing, and having a good time.

Just then Chad leaned over, put his arm around me, and said, "Dad, how about those Cowboys?"

Touchdown! We embraced and turned our attention back to George.

Then it hit me. It doesn't matter how you say "I love you" as long as you say it. Chad's language of love suddenly became my own. We had the joy of communicating that special love.

I stood tall that night. I sang, laughed, and almost cried. In that moment, the Lord spoke to my heart, *How about that, cowboy?*

❧

LOVELY MORNINGS, LOVELY DAYS. . .

Once there was a Dad
And he loved a little boy
And every day the boy would come
And climb into Dad's place in bed
And giggle.
The boy would hide deep under the covers
And shout, "What's this lump in your bed?"
And cuddle with his puppy
And make a morning so lovely
It would inevitably last the whole day.

And the Dad loved the boy,
Very much. . .

❧

THE LOVELIEST WOMAN
OF THE TWENTIETH CENTURY

The loveliest woman of the twentieth century was not a supermodel or a princess, not a glamorous actress or a championship sports figure, not even a pop star or a beauty pageant winner. Rather, in our opinion at least, the loveliest person who lived during the 1900s was a frail old woman named Agnes.

Let us describe her for you. She stood only four feet, eleven inches tall. She weighed less than a hundred pounds, and (to be honest) her face often resembled a shriveled prune. She never owned a home or a car or even so much as a closet full of clothes. As a nineteen-year-old girl, she took the name of Mary Teresa and dedicated her life to serving Jesus as a nun. Perhaps you know her best by the name she earned later in life, Mother Teresa.

And what did Mother Teresa do that made her the most beautiful person of the twentieth century? Simply this: She cared for the sick and dying.

In fact, she was often called the "Saint of the

Gutters" because she was always willing to help people the rest of the world despised. In her hometown of Calcutta, India, she often patrolled the streets looking for the "poorest of the poor," finding the terminally ill in the streets and literally carrying them from the gutters to Nirmal Hriday, her "home for the dying" where these people could die with dignity.

Perhaps the best way to view the beauty of Mother Teresa is through the lens of a story from her life. The time was 1955. Leaving Nirmal Hriday one time, she happened upon a Hindu priest outside her door. In the months prior, many Hindu believers in Calcutta had been harassing Teresa and the other nuns assisting her, determined to oust these Christian nuns from their city. They'd thrown stones and insults at the nuns, and even threatened to kill Teresa. By all rights, Mother Teresa should have harbored hatred toward Hindus, and particularly toward Hindu leaders like this priest.

But that day all Mother Teresa saw was a man, lying on the pavement, literally dying in his own vomit. He was a victim of the deadly disease cholera. Because cholera is highly contagious, none of his fellow Hindu believers would touch him, gathering instead to form a crowd that watched in fascinated horror as this Hindu priest began to die an agonizing death.

Mother Teresa didn't hesitate. Pushing her

way through the crowd, the little woman picked up the priest and carried him in her arms back inside Nirmal Hriday. There, she carefully placed him in a clean bed, then washed the refuse from his face and body. His death came soon after, but thanks to this Christian nun, the Hindu priest was allowed to die with dignity, his body clean and resting in a clean bed.

Each day of Mother Teresa's life contained these kind of simple, selfless acts of beauty and service, so much so that when she died, she was mourned by princes and paupers alike. And because of her life, we are all changed, all given glimpse after glimpse of true beauty: Jesus Himself. For that reason we can think of no lovelier woman from the modern age, none who lived a life with more daily beauty than this little nun they once called Agnes.

We look forward to meeting her in heaven one day, and when we do, we'll utter only one word.

"Thanks."

❧

A Prayer for a Lovely Day

Author Unknown

I will not hurry through this day!
Lord, I will listen by the way,

To humming bees and singing birds,
To speaking trees and friendly words;
And for the moments in between
Seek glimpses of the great Unseen.
I will not hurry through this day!
I will take time to think and pray!
I will look into the sky,
Where fleecy clouds and swallows fly;
And somewhere in the day, maybe,
I will catch whispers, Lord, from Thee.

❧

*When all is said and done, it's not what's
outside that makes one lovely, but what is
inside. . .*

THE LETTER

The lady caught her breath when she saw the letter. A smile sneaked onto her lips when she saw the name attached to it. It was from her love, her fiancé now so far from his home in England. He had gone to the colonies to fight for the Crown in what the Americans were calling "The Revolutionary War."

Before he left, he'd made his love known, and the soldier and the lady had joyously agreed to marry. They would wed after the war and live happily ever after, she was sure.

The lady hurried her way to a private place

and gently tore open the page from her love. At first the smile froze on her face, then, wearily, it crept away completely and was soon replaced by tears.

The words on the page revealed a man in great pain, both physical and emotional. He had been wounded, he said, during battle. Badly wounded. In fact, he had lost a leg completely, and in his eyes had become less than a man.

"I am disfigured and maimed," he wrote, "and so changed from when you last saw me." And he then released her from her pledge to marry, breaking off their engagement and urging her to find another man. A whole man. . .

The soldier caught his breath when he saw the letter. In truth, he had longed for it to come, but felt certain it never would. And he feared its coming as well, for it could only mean tears. But he clutched it anyway. It was from the lady he loved and had once pledged to marry, the Englishwoman who vowed to wait through a war for him.

She is so beautiful, he thought, remembering her hair, her smile, the gentle touch of her hand. *And she is no longer mine.*

Silently, he ripped open the note, a frown upon his face. At first the frown froze there, then, quietly, it crept away completely and was soon replaced with a smile.

She is so beautiful, he thought, remembering nothing of her appearance and instead gazing deeply into her heart. For in the letter she spoke again of her love, hotly denying the suggestion that she would end her engagement to the now-crippled soldier.

He read the letter once more, stopping on the line that held his heart. "I will marry you," his lady wrote firmly, "as long as there is enough body left to hold your soul."

6

Whatever Is

Admirable

ADMIRABLE: (adjective) (1) deserving the highest esteem; (2) exciting wonder. Synonyms: worthy, commendable, esteemed, respectable, meritorious.

A Dog's Life

The story is told of a certain man who liked to travel, and his favorite traveling companion was his dog. Realizing that hotel employees sometimes frown upon guests bringing pets, he wrote ahead to the manager of a hotel he planned to stay at and asked whether or not they allowed animals in their rooms. This was the manager's reply:

> *Dear Sir:*
> *I've been in the hotel business over thirty years. Never yet have I called the police to eject a disorderly dog during the small hours of the night. Never yet has a dog set the bedclothes afire from smoking a cigarette. I've never found a hotel towel or blanket in a dog's suitcase, nor whiskey rings on the bureau top from a dog's bottle.*
> *Sure the dog's welcome.*
> *The Manager*
>
> *P.S. If he'll vouch for you, come along, too.*

AMERICA IS GREAT
BECAUSE SHE IS GOOD

by Alexis de Tocqueville

I sought for the greatness
and genius of America
in her commodious harbors
and her ample rivers,
and it was not there;

in the fertile fields
and boundless prairies,
and it was not there;

in her rich mines
and her vast world commerce,
and it was not there.

Not until I went
into the churches of America
and heard her pulpits,
aflame with righteousness,
did I understand the secret
of her genius and power.

America is great
because she is good,
and if America ever ceases to be good,
America will cease to be great.

THE MAKING OF A ROLE MODEL

Perhaps you've heard of LL Cool J. He's a multi-talented individual, a pioneer of rap/hip-hop music, an accomplished actor, and more. Immensely popular, he's sold millions of records and impacted millions more teenagers and young adults who've come to admire the man and his music.

Now, don't get me wrong. LL Cool J is no saint. Far from it, in fact. He strikes me as a troubled man, full of fury and vulgarity—and his songs reflect that. Although I respect his ability as an artist, I can't deny the powerful negative influence he's had on America's children—including attitudes, clothing styles, musical tastes, and more. Unfortunately, I stand against much of what he stands for.

Still, this artist caught my attention recently with one of his songs. I heard it while skimming down the radio dial in my car. It's called simply "Father." This tune, full of bass beat and funky background vocals, captured me in a way I can't explain. You see, LL Cool J was talking about his childhood, revealing something about what shaped him into the man he is today.

When he was four years old, his parents split up. His mother left, actually, to escape a physically abusive husband. Not long after, the boy's father got drunk and decided to take out his rage on LL Cool J's mother. He loaded a shotgun, caught his mother on her way home from work, and shot her in the back. Also shot the boy's grandfather. Ten times. LL Cool J never saw his father again.

Mother and grandfather survived, eventually returning to normal life. LL Cool J's mother even kindled a new romance, bringing a stepfather of sorts home to her son.

You've heard the saying "Beaten like a step-child"? That's what this boy endured in the ensuing years. Beaten with belts. Kicked down a flight of stairs. Punched in the chest. Stomped upon. Thrown outside into cold, hard snow.

"Late at night on my knees I pray, young child wishing, the pain would go away," the artist raps today. And then comes the chorus that so sobered me, "All I ever wanted; all I ever needed; was a father; That's all."

When I hear this song even now, I don't see a millionaire gansta rapper, angry and violent and irreverent and disgustingly crude. I see a boy sitting bruised and beaten by his bed, wishing, longing, aching for his father. A father who never comes.

I often wonder to myself how this rap singer, this American role model, might be different if his father had managed to control his anger, if he had come to know Jesus personally, intimately. If he had been the kind of father this disillusioned boy could have admired. If he'd spent his days and nights with his son modeling for him the Father in heaven.

And it makes me realize who the real role models in America are today. They are the men and women, the mothers and fathers and grandparents and uncles and aunts and cousins and brothers and sisters who live their lives in such ways that their younger family members can say, "When I grow up, I want to be just like that."

Then, like LL Cool J, those children, too, can grow up and take prominent places in society— and, unlike LL Cool J, lead people away from hatred and pain instead of toward it.

And I notice that in spite of himself, LL Cool J has done something admirable with his music. He's made me (and I hope you) realize how very important our lives are to those children around us. He's helped me remember that I (like you) am a role model to my kids, so I'd better start behaving like a good one.

I think I'll start today.

A Prayer for Role Models— and Their Followers

by Thomas à Kempis

Grant, O Lord, to all teachers and students, to know what is worth knowing, to love what is worth loving, to praise what pleases You most, and to dislike whatsoever is evil in Your sight. Grant us with true judgment to distinguish things that differ, and above all to search out and do what is well-pleasing to You, through Jesus Christ our Lord.

❧

As John Duckworth deftly illustrates in this next story, we are often mistaken about what is admirable and what is not!

A Pocketful of Change*

by John Duckworth

Once upon a time there was a man who had a pocketful of change.

It wasn't a big pocketful, but the man thought it was enough. After all, hadn't he chosen each coin long ago? Hadn't he paid dearly for each one? Now he could use them to accomplish his purposes.

Or so he thought.

"Let's see," he said, reaching into his pocket. "How much have I got here?" He counted the coins into his palm. "One nickel, three dimes, a penny, two quarters, a fifty-cent piece, and a silver dollar." He smiled. "Good! Now I can use them to buy the things I need."

So off he went down the street, whistling happily. He whistled so loudly, in fact, that he couldn't hear the tiny, tinny racket that was coming from his pocket.

"I don't like it in here," the fifty-cent piece was saying. "It's too crowded and stuffy. And I don't like having to associate with coins of lower denominations."

"Look who's talking," said the silver dollar. "I'm worth twice your value. You're just overweight."

One of the quarters scoffed. "You're both out of date," he said. "You're useless in today's vending machine world. People much prefer our slim, sleek shapes. Why don't you go back to the mint where you came from?"

The dollar glared. "Well, at least we're not dimes. They're the smallest coins of all and the easiest to lose. Not that they'd be missed, mind you."

"Size isn't everything!" said the dimes in chorus. "Each of us is worth twice as much as that chubby nickel."

"Well," the nickel said, indignant. "You're forgetting the lowliest coin of all. I'm glad I'm not a penny. A penny can't buy anything anymore!"

The penny, who couldn't think of anything clever to say, blushed a coppery red. All the other coins laughed at him.

Finally, the penny sighed. "I guess you're right," he said. "I don't know why the man bothers to carry me around in this pocket. I'm worthless to him. He could never use me to buy anything he needed." The others noisily agreed, clinking and snickering and saying that he wasn't worth a plugged nickel.

Meanwhile, the man had whistled and walked so far that he was getting hungry. Soon he came to a vending machine that sold candy bars.

"I am getting hungry," he said, "and those candy bars do look good. I think I'll use my two quarters to get a snack." With that he reached into his pocket.

"Oh, no, you don't!" the quarters said, too faintly for the man to hear. They burrowed deeper into the pocket. "No one's going to take us out of our nice, warm home. We'll hide down here until that hand goes away. Let the man use some other coin."

But no other coin would fit the man's purpose. So he dug deeper—and the deeper he dug, the deeper the quarters burrowed. Before long, the quarters found a little hole in the bottom of the man's pocket.

"Aha!" the quarters cried. "Here's our chance to escape. Now we can get away from the man and spend our lives as we please!" Pushing with all their might, the quarters forced their way through the little hole.

"We're free!" they cried, falling unnoticed to the sidewalk. "We can go anywhere, do anything we want!" But they found themselves rolling out of control, spinning into the gutter. With a splish they hit the dirty water and lay helpless, their shiny faces pointed at the sky.

The man sighed, pulling his hand from his pocket. "I thought I had two quarters," he said. "But I guess not." Still hungry, he continued down the street.

In the pocket, one of the dimes was getting an idea. "Hey," he said. "I'm tired of always being put down because of my size. I've never liked being a dime anyway. Let's turn ourselves into quarters!"

"Yeah!" said the other two dimes. "Quarters get a lot more attention. Since those two left, the man is bound to need some more. Won't he be impressed with how important we are!"

So the dimes gathered all their strength. They puffed themselves up, trying to look like quarters.

Just then the man came to a telephone booth.

"I've got to make a call," he said. "And those three dimes in my pocket will help me do it."

He dug into his pocket and pulled out the dimes, who were still puffing themselves up, holding their breaths, pretending to be quarters. But they still looked like dimes. "Ah," the man said, "there you are. I'll just put the three of you into this pay phone so I can make that important call."

"What?" the dimes cried to each other in their tiny voices. "Why, we've never been so insulted! Can't he see that our true calling is to be quarters? Who does he think he is, anyway, restricting our self-worth?" With that they wriggled from the man's fingers and fell to the sidewalk.

"We'll find someone who appreciates our real value," the dimes sniffed. But like the quarters, they rolled into the gutter where the man couldn't find them.

"My, my," the man said, sighing again. "None of the other coins is useful to me in making this phone call. I guess I'll have to go into a store and get change for my fifty-cent piece." So he entered the next store on the street.

"Whoa!" the fifty-cent piece growled from deep in the man's pocket. "He's not going to exchange me for inferior coins. I hate lying in a dark cash register drawer with all those strangers. I'm a big, important coin, and I want to stay that way!" Grunting and squeezing, the fifty-cent piece worked his way through the little hole in the man's pocket and fell to the floor. There he rolled under a counter, lost in the dust.

"Help," he cried weakly. But no one could hear.

The man rummaged in his pocket. "I was sure I had a fifty-cent piece," he told the cashier. "But I guess not." He thought for a moment. "Maybe I could use my silver dollar to get change. I'll just get twice as much, that's all."

The dollar roared a miniature roar. "Never!" he said. "I'm not going to be anybody's second choice. I'm the most valuable coin there is! I should be kept safe in the bank, not left to tarnish in this dump!" Harrumphing, the dollar coin slipped through the hole in the pocket and tried to leap onto the counter. But he fell short, plunging into a nearby trash can. There he blustered and fumed—but couldn't budge.

"I guess I don't have a silver dollar after all," the man said sadly, finding none in his pocket. Apologizing to the clerk, he left the store.

The man walked and walked and walked. Finally he reached the spot where he'd parked his car. There he saw a meter maid putting a parking ticket on his windshield.

"Wait," the man cried. "I have a nickel I can put in the parking meter. I'll just get it out of my pocket—"

"No way!" the nickel protested. "You're not

spending me on some parking meter. I have higher ambitions. I want to help build a great big hospital or buy a fancy new yacht!"

The nickel jumped through the hole—only to fall under a car's muddy tire, stuck.

"I guess I don't have that nickel either," the man said, shaking his head. The meter maid handed him the parking ticket and drove away.

The man sighed once more. "Well," he said. "I thought I had a whole pocketful of change to use. But all I've got now is no candy bar, no phone call, a parking ticket, and no money. Except, that is, for this little penny."

The penny, who had been clinging desperately to the man's pocket so as not to slip through the hole in the bottom, sighed with relief as the man's fingers took hold of him. "Oh, use me!" the penny cried. "Maybe you could use me to buy a gum ball. I'm afraid I'm not good for much else."

The man brought the penny close to his eyes. "Hmm," he said, looking and frowning. Then he turned the penny over. "Aha!" he exclaimed, his frown turning to a smile. Holding the penny firmly in his hand, he whistled and walked down the street. The penny, unable to see or hear, waited breathlessly to find out whether the man could find a way to use him.

Finally the man stopped walking. Moments later the penny could see and hear again—and discovered he was lying on a counter in a store. It was a very nice store. Looking up, the penny saw a sign on the wall.

RARE COINS BOUGHT AND SOLD, the sign said.

"That's a valuable penny, all right," a kind-looking lady behind the counter was saying to the man. "1909-S VDB. It's worth about two hundred dollars!"

The penny gasped, "I—I am?" he asked. "I am?"

So it happened that the man, who knew a great deal about coins, sold the little penny for quite a bit of money. The penny, who was happy as could be, was displayed in a place of honor— in an elegant glass case—and the man had enough money to get all the candy bars and phone calls he could want and pay his parking ticket, too.

The other coins? They just sat in their gutters and dust, wondering why no one ever used them anymore.

"No one recognizes how valuable we are," they said crossly. "After all, we're not a bunch of pennies or something!"

They lived unhappily ever after.

Speaking of Admiration. . .

"Nothing great was ever achieved without great men, and men are great only if they are determined to be so."   CHARLES DE GAULLE, as quoted by CHARLES HENNING in *The Wit and Wisdom of Politics*

"Tell me who admires you and loves you, and I will tell who you are."
CHARLES AUGUSTIN SAINTE-BEAUVE, as recorded on Quoteland.com

"My mother, a Jewish immigrant from Lithuania, used to tell her seven kids, 'All my children are excellent. What's the big deal? Go do some good in the world and I'll be impressed.' "
MORTON ABRAMOWITZ, as quoted by LORNE A. ADRAIN in *The Most Important Thing I Know*

"Admire a big horse. Saddle a small one."
Cowboy proverb, as recorded by KEN ALSTAD in *Savvy Sayin's*

"There is nothing nobler or more admirable than when two people who see eye to eye keep house as man and wife, confounding their enemies and delighting their friends."   HOMER, as quoted on Quoteworld.eilc.org

"For every heart love has healed,
every hope faith makes real,
in all these things,
oh I have seen the hand of God"
RANDY STONEHILL, in the song
"Hand of God" on the album *Thirst*

"We all have a responsibility to be role models. As parents, as brothers and sisters, as aunts and uncles, grandparents, whoever. It's our responsibility to do the right thing. I take my position as a Christian role model and as a professional athlete very seriously and I try and do the right thing all the time."

NFL player CHAD HENNINGS,
in a *Nappaland Communications, Inc.* interview

"You seem a decent fellow,
I hate to kill you."
INIGO MONTOYA
(portrayed by MANDY PATINKIN),
admiring his opponent just before
a swordfight in *The Princess Bride*

"Love is the most difficult and dangerous form of courage. Courage is the most desperate, admirable, and noble kind of love."

DELMORE SCHWARTZ,
as quoted on Quoteworld.eilc.org

"My religion consists of a humble admiration of the unlimitable superior who reveals Himself in the slight details we are able to perceive with our frail and feeble minds."

ALBERT EINSTEIN,
as quoted on Aphids.com

❧

THE WORD ON WHAT'S ADMIRABLE. . .

This is how we know what love is:
Jesus Christ laid down his life for us.
And we ought to lay down our lives
for our brothers.
1 JOHN 3:16 NIV

The unfailing love of the LORD never ends! By his mercies we have been kept from complete destruction. Great is his faithfulness; his mercies begin afresh each day.

LAMENTATIONS 3:22–23 NLT

Let no one look down on your youthfulness,
but rather in speech, conduct,
love, faith and purity,
show yourself an example of
those who believe.
1 TIMOTHY 4:12 NASB

But be holy in all you do, just as God, the One who called you, is holy. It is written in the Scriptures: "You must be holy, because I am holy."

1 PETER 1:15–16 NCV

Set your mind on things above,
not on things on the earth.
COLOSSIANS 3:2 NKJV

❧

Christian music artist Steven Curtis Chapman is a hero to many, admired by millions who've made him an award-winning and best-selling musician. In his excellent book Speechless *(co-authored with Scotty Smith), Steven Curtis Chapman shares about one of his heroes, a man he admires and tries to emulate. Listen as he tells more about that person here. . .*

GRACE IS SO MUCH MORE THAN A WORD*

by Steven Curtis Chapman

I have had the privilege of meeting some extraordinary Christian leaders, but none has made a greater impression on me than Chuck Colson. God brought us together, and it has been my honor to invest time and heart in the work of Prison Fellowship. Chuck has enabled me to take my music into many prison facilities during the course of my concert tours—but that's the easiest thing he has done for me.

My first encounter with Chuck came through his book *Loving God.* I can still remember being riveted to each page as I read about his experiences of going behind prison walls and sharing the grace of God through cell bars with those awaiting their fate on death row. As I read, I thought, *God, how do You work in a man's heart to give him that kind of bold love? If only I could walk alongside such a man of faith in a death-row cell block someday, but that will never happen.* Oh me of little faith!

Later, as I worked on ideas for my album *Heaven in the Real World,* I came across some quotes by Chuck that gave me an idea for a couple of songs. I longed for an opportunity to speak with him directly and get some of his input on the themes I felt compelled to write about.

Then one day the phone rang. My heart skipped a beat, because a phone conversation had been arranged between Chuck's office and mine, and I suspected that this was his call coming in.

"Hello, Steven. This is Chuck Colson calling."

"Hello, Mr. Colson. Thank you so much for

taking the time to talk with me. This is a real honor for me."

"Please, Steven, call me Chuck."

Thus began a wonderful friendship—and Chuck's mentoring continues to shape the way I think about life and ministry. And to think that I had been afraid to even hope for such an opportunity. God truly does give good gifts.

It was a bright sunny day as I emptied my pockets before passing through the metal detectors. No, I was not boarding a plane for yet another concert date. I stood at the entrance to the Michigan City Correctional Institute, a maximum security prison in Northern Indiana. I felt both excited and nervous as I anticipated visiting death row for the first time. Every preconceived image of life within prison I had obtained from film, news clips, and a child's imagination ran through my mind.

"Steven!" I heard the ring of that familiar voice from across the room.

"Hi, Chuck, how are you?" It still felt kind of strange calling this hero of the faith of mine by his first name, but it also felt reassuring to know I was with a friend. He explained that prior to our worship service on the prison yard, we would be visiting inmates on death row, including one man who had become a Christian forty years earlier. The ministry of Prison Fellowship had become a primary means of discipleship and nurture for him, even as Chuck had become one of his best friends.

I stayed close to my new buddy and mentor as he navigated our way through the series of iron-gated entries. Each set of doors would electronically open and then close behind us before the next set would do the same. What an eerie feeling. Eventually we began our journey down the long hallway lined with cells inhabited by sons, fathers, [and] grandfathers who were paying the price for some terrible crime committed.

I watched my teacher intently as he offered grace to those we encountered. Whether it was simply a smile, a word, a handshake through the bars, and many times a prayer. Chuck was showing me what it means to treat all men with dignity and respect. I'm not sure I have ever met anyone who can so freely love in the most difficult of situations a segment of society that appears to be so unlovable.

I tried to emulate him as I grew a little more confident. I listened to the sad lament of a grandfather who showed me the pictures of his grandchildren whom he had wounded deeply with his tragic choices. Together, Chuck and I prayed with one African-American brother who greeted us with a smile and a joy that could only be traced to the life-giving grace of God. He, like many others, spoke with great remorse and sorrow for the lives of those affected most by the evil they had done, namely, the victims and their loved ones. This brother went on to tell us how God had given him life and freedom even though he was deserving of death. He told us how he had been and would continue to be praying for us as we carried the gospel to others inside of prison, as well as those outside the stone walls. In some ways he seemed to be a whole lot more free in his prison cell than many of us who will never see the inside of such a prison.

Our cell block walk culminated with a visit to Chuck's friend, Bob (not his real name), inside a heavily secured room. I would describe it as the equivalent of a large iron-caged room inside two other iron cages. Bob was a large man, and when he shuffled into the room in shackles and hand-cuffs I felt a surge of fear come over me. How-ever, as we all talked, I only saw the evidence of a man who had been changed from death to life. I watched as Chuck and Bob embraced for the first time without handcuffs impeding their hug. The three of us then wrapped arms around each other in a circle and thanked God for His love. What else could level the ground in such a pro-found way that one of the great Christian leaders of our time, a death-row inmate, and a Christian songwriter could come together before the throne of the living God as brothers, one in Christ?

This first trip proved to be one of the most profound experiences of the awesome reality of

God's grace I have ever encountered. It also helped me further define the kind of men and women whom I want to follow as they follow Christ. The events of that day inspired me to write a song called "Free" which was included on my *Signs of Life* album. Knowing Chuck and getting to visit many correctional institutions since that first visit only deepen my desire for God to free my heart to love all men as He loves me in His Son.

❧

Contrary to popular opinion, it takes more than just a flashy personality and a few worn-out catchphrases to be a truly admirable role model. Don't believe us? Then read on to discover what happened to one such would-be superman in the brief comedy called. . .

INSPIRATIONAL GUY AND THE ETERNAL PESSIMIST SOCIETY

THE SCENE
A meeting of the Eternal Pessimist Society.

Inspirational Guy—A superhero; male

Poetry Girl—Inspirational Guy's superhero sidekick; female

Eeyore 1—President of the Eternal Pessimist Society

Eeyore 2—Member of the Eternal Pessimist Society

Eeyore 3—Member of the Eternal Pessimist Society

Eeyore 4—Member of the Eternal Pessimist Society

PROP/SETUP

You'll need seven chairs set in a semicircle at center stage and a large sign saying "Eternal Pessimist Society Meets Here (If Anybody Shows Up)" hanging behind the chairs. You'll also need an Eeyore stuffed animal, a notebook for Eeyore 1, and basic superhero outfits (capes, masks, and insignias) for Inspirational Guy and Poetry Girl.

THE SCRIPT
*"Inspirational Guy and
the Eternal Pessimist Society"*

(Scene opens with an empty stage, except for the seven chairs and large sign. The stuffed Eeyore is seated in the center chair. One by one, the human Eeyores enter and take their seats.

Throughout the entire skit, all Eeyores should speak in an annoying monotone)

Eeyore 1: (Enters from stage right. Looks around and shakes his or her head in disgust.) Just as I expected. I'm the only one to show up for the meeting. (Takes a seat.)

Eeyore 2: (Enters from stage left. Looks around and shakes his or her head in disgust.) Just as I expected. (Motions at Eeyore 1.) You're here. (Sighs, and takes a seat.)

Eeyore 3: (Enters from stage left. Looks around and shakes his or her head in disgust.) I knew it. (Motions at Eeyores 1 and 2.) You two are here. (Sighs, and takes a seat.)

Eeyore 4: (Enters from stage left. Looks around and shakes his or her head in disgust.) It figures. (Motions at Eeyore 1, 2, and 3.) Of all people, I'm always the last one to show up. (Sighs, and takes a seat.)

Eeyore 1: (Stands and sighs.) Well, it probably won't do any good, but let's open the meeting with our rousing Eternal Pessimist cheer. (Leading cheer in monotone.) Gimme an E.

Eeyores 2, 3, 4: (Equally unexcited.) E.

Eeyore 1: (Sighs.) Gimme another E.

Eeyores 2, 3, 4: (Still bland.) E.

Eeyore 1: Gimme a Y.

Eeyores 2, 3, 4: Y.

Eeyore 1: Gimme an O, R, E.

Eeyores 2, 3, 4: O. R. E.

Eeyore 1: What's that spell?

Eeyores 2, 3, 4: Eeyore. Eeyore. Eeyore. Hooray.

Eeyore 1: (Sitting.) See. I told you it wouldn't do any good. (Looks at watch.) okay. Time for our Optimist Exercise. I'll read a situation, and you respond. Ready? (Reading from a notebook.) The weather report says it's going to be sunny tomorrow.

Eeyore 2: (Raising hand.) Two words: "Sunburn City." (All others nod and mumble in agreement.)

Eeyore 1: Number 2: You just won millions in the lottery.

Eeyore 3: I'll take this one. (Counting off each one on his fingers.) Taxes. Mugging. Crooked accountant. More taxes. Stock market crash. Price hike in Underoos. Great Aunt Daisy and her lifelong dream of owning the Rolling Stones rock band. Huge fire that burns the mattress where you keep your cash winnings. Chapter 11. Death.

Eeyore 4: (Whispering to Eeyore 2) Wow. He's good.

Eeyore 1: Well, I have more situations, but I don't really see the point of reading them anymore. Why don't we sit here until this meeting is over. Or until we die. Whichever comes first.

(All Eeyores nod in solemn agreement, then stare into space, oblivious to anything around them. After a moment, Inspirational Guy and Poetry Girl burst into the room. They are full of energy and positivity—an obvious contrast to the people already in the room. The Eeyores ignore the entrance.)

Inspirational Guy: (Blocking Poetry Girl) Have no fear, Inspirational Guy is here!

Poetry Girl: (Elbowing her way into view) And yes, it's true! Poetry Girl came, too!

Inspirational Guy: (Surveys the scene.) Oh no, Poetry Girl! We're too late! They've gone senseless with hopelessness already! My vast powers of inspiration are useless! (Snapping his fingers as he turns to leave) And I had a really good story about a spider and a pig. I was gonna call the spider Charlotte, and the pig Wilbur, and. . .

Poetry Girl: (Perky as ever) There, there I.G.; Look around—what do you see?

Inspirational Guy: (Looks around. Spots the stuffed Eeyore.) Cool! A stuffed Eeyore. (Reaches over and picks up the stuffed Eeyore.) Ever see that episode where Eeyore's tail comes off, and Christopher Robin gets his trusty hammer, and. . .

All Eeyores: (In monotone, appalled that anyone would dare touch the society mascot.) Aaaaaaaauuuuugggghhh. (Inspirational Guy gently returns the stuffed Eeyore to its chair.)

Eeyore 1: Figures.

Eeyore 2: Of all the Eternal Pessimist Society meetings, we get the one with inspirational superheroes who have no respect for a role model.

Eeyore 3: And to think, I could have been home drinking prune juice out of a tennis shoe tonight.

Inspirational Guy: (Full of enthusiasm, with a hand cupped around one ear, and a tad melodramatic) Hark! I hear the mournful cries of people without hope! Be hopeless no more! Inspirational Guy is here! As the timeless song goes, (singing out of tune and at the top of his lungs) "Just what makes that little old ant think he can move a some kind of really big plant. . ." (Struggling for the words, but singing anyway) and some more words I can't quite remember. . .ba dee dum. . . . Oh well. . . skip to the chorus. . . . "He's got hiiiigh hopes! He's got, hiiiiigh hopes. . ."

Eeyore 4: (Tapping Poetry Girl on the shoulder) Does he always leave you out when he introduces himself?

Poetry Girl: (A little surprised, then slightly annoyed) Well. . .um. . .yeah. (Remembering she's supposed to rhyme) I mean. . . . Well, yes, my friend! This oversight never does end! (Frowns.)

Inspirational Guy: (Clearing throat) Um, Poetry Girl. If you can't be quiet, I'll have to separate you two. (Returning attention to the Eeyores) Okay. Enough of the song. (Rubbing hands together in gleeful anticipation) Have I got a story for you! (Very dramatic) Once there was this pig and his friend, a spider.

Eeyore 3: (Raising hand to stop Inspirational Guy) Heard it. Spider dies. 'Nuff said.

Poetry Girl: (Shocked and near tears) The spider dies! This makes me cry—uh, cries! (Frowning at Inspirational Guy) What kind of inspirational superhero are you? One that makes everyone feel blue?

Inspirational Guy: (Refusing to give up) Okay. Bad story. Forget I ever mentioned it. But listen, you guys need a positive role model, and I'm gonna give it to you—whether you like it or not. Let's see, song bombed. Story's a no-go. Time for the heavy artillery—inspirational quotes! (Thinking) Ahh, yes. As Shakespeare once said, (Dramatic) "Love alters not with his brief hours and weeks. . ."

Eeyore 2: (Raising hand to stop Inspirational Guy) Excuse me. Would that be William Shakespeare? (Inspirational Guy nods, smiling.)

Eeyore 3: He's dead. (Poetry Girl looks shocked and chokes back a sob. Eeyore 3 shrugs and looks almost sympathetically at Poetry Girl.) Could be worse.

Eeyore 4: Yeah. He could have a bee sting behind his left ear.

Eeyore 1: Or a piece of meat stuck between his teeth for all eternity.

Eeyore 2: Or be trapped in a Gilligan's Island episode where the Skipper is locked in some kind of endless, snoring coma.

Eeyore 3: Or he could be here listening to inspirational stories from some costumed superguy who ignores his sidekick.

Poetry Girl: (Glaring at Inspirational Guy) Humph. (Mimicking Inspirational Guy) "Be a superhero," you said. "Spread a little hope in darkened lives," you said. "Be the kind of person people can look up to and admire," you said. Then all you do is ignore me while you talk about dead people! (Tearing off her mask and kicking Inspirational Guy in the shins) That's it. I quit! From now on, I'm joining the Eternal Pessimist Society.

Eeyore 1: (Rolling his or her eyes) Great. Just what we need. Another Pessimist to feed.

Eeyore 4: Yeah. And she'll probably want my chair.

Eeyore 2: And she'll probably want to tell me

all about her former happy life as a super-girl. (Shivers.)

Eeyore 3: And then she'll die. (Poetry Girl runs out, sobbing.)

Inspirational Guy: (Torn between following Poetry Girl and staying to duke it out with the Eeyores) Hey! That wasn't nice.

Eeyore 3: (Shrugging shoulders) Could've been worse.

Eeyore 4: Yeah. Like she could have had a bee sting behind her left ear.

Eeyore 1: Or a piece of meat stuck between her teeth for all eternity.

Inspirational Guy: (Covering his ears) No! Stop! I give up! "He who fights and runs away, lives to fight another day!" (Runs off-stage, screaming.)

Eeyore 1: (After a moment) So. Might as well sit and stare into space. (Sighs.) Can't think of anything better to do. (Other Eeyores shrug and join him. Lights go out to signal end.)

❧

Two Surprises

Author Unknown

A workman plied his clumsy spade
As the sun was going down;

The German king with his cavalcade
Was coming into town.
The king stopped short when he saw the
    man.
"My worthy friend," said he,
"Why not cease work at eventide,
When the laborer should be free?"

"I do not slave," the old man said,
"And I am always free;
Though I work from the time I leave my bed
Till I can hardly see."

"How much," said the king, "is thy gain
    in a day?"
"Eight groschen," the man replied.
"And canst thou live on this meager pay?"
"Like a king," he said with pride.

"Two groschen for me and my wife,
    good friend,
And two for a debt I owe;
Two groschen to lend and two to spend
For those who can't labor, you know."

"Thy debt?" said the king. Said the toiler,
    "Yea,
To my mother with age oppressed,
Who cared for me, toiled for me,
    many a day,

And now hath need of rest."
"To whom dost lend of thy daily store?"
"To my three boys at school. You see,
When I am too feeble to toil anymore,
They will care for their mother and me."

"And thy last two groschen?" the monarch
said.
"My sisters are old and lame;
I give them two groschen for raiment and
bread,
All in the Father's name."

Tears welled up in the good king's eyes.
"Thou knowest me not," said he;
"As thou hast given me one surprise,
Here is another for thee.

"I am thy king; give me thy hand."
And he heaped it high with gold.
"When more thou needest, I command
That I at once be told.

"For I would bless with rich reward
The man who can proudly say,
That eight souls he doth keep and guard
On eight poor groschen a day."

In his timeless book No Wonder They Call Him the Savior, *Max Lucado eloquently described a life lived admirably— the life of his father. We feel honored to close this chapter with Max's words for you here. . .*

FINAL WORDS, FINAL ACTS*

by Max Lucado

In a recent trip to my hometown I took some time to go see a tree. "A live oak tree," my dad had called it (with the accent on "live"). It was nothing more than a sapling, so thin I could wrap my hands around it and touch my middle finger to my thumb. The West Texas wind scattered the fall leaves and caused me to zip up my coat. There is nothing colder than a prairie wind, especially in a cemetery.

"A special tree," I said to myself, "with a special job." I looked around. The cemetery was lined with elms but no oaks. The ground was dotted with tombstones but no trees. Just this one. A special tree for a special man.

About three years ago Daddy began noticing a steady weakening of his muscles. It began in his hands. He then felt it in his calves. Next his arms thinned a bit.

He mentioned his condition to my brother-in-law, who is a physician. My brother-in-law, alarmed, sent him to a specialist. The specialist conducted a lengthy battery of tests—blood, neurological, and muscular—and he reached his conclusion. Lou Gehrig's disease. A devastating crippler. No one knows the cause or the cure. The only sure thing about it is its cruelty and accuracy.

I looked down at the plot of ground that would someday entomb my father. Daddy always wanted to be buried under an oak tree, so he bought this one. "Special order from the valley," he had boasted. "Had to get special permission from the city council to put it here." (That wasn't hard in this dusty oil field town where everybody knows everybody.)

The lump got tighter in my throat. A lesser man might have been angry. Another man might have given up. But Daddy didn't. He knew that his days were numbered so began to get his house in order.

The tree was only one of the preparations he made. He improved the house for Mom by installing a sprinkler system and garage door opener and by painting the trim. He got the will updated. He verified the insurance and retirement policies. He bought some stock toward his grandchildren's education. He planned his funeral. He bought cemetery plots for himself and Mom.

He prepared his kids through words of assurance and letters of love. And last of all, he bought the tree. A live oak tree. (Pronounced with an accent on "live.")

Final acts. Final hours. Final words.

They reflect a life well lived. So do the last words of our Master. When on the edge of death, Jesus, too, got His house in order:

A final prayer of forgiveness.
A plea honored.
A request of love.
A question of suffering.
A confession of humanity.
A call of deliverance.
A cry of completion.

Words of chance muttered by a desperate martyr? No. Words of intent, painted by the Divine Deliverer on the canvas of sacrifice.

Final words. Final acts. Each one is a window through which the cross can be better understood. Each one opens a treasury of promises. "So that is where you learned it," I said aloud as though speaking to my father. I smiled to myself and thought, *It's much easier to die like Jesus if you have lived like Him for a lifetime.*

The final hours are passing now. The gentle flame on his candle grows weaker and weaker. He lies in peace. His body dying, his spirit living.

No longer can he get out of bed. He has chosen to live his last days at home. It won't be long. Death's windy draft will soon exhaust the flickering candle and it will be over.

I looked one last time at the slender oak. I touched it as if it had been hearing my thoughts. "Grow," I whispered. "Grow strong. Stand tall. Yours is a valued treasure."

As I drove home through the ragged oil field patchwork, I kept thinking about that tree. Though feeble, the decades will find it strong. Though slender, the years will add thickness and strength. Its last years will be its best. Just like my father's. Just like my Master's. "It is much easier to die like Jesus if you have lived like Him for a lifetime."

"Grow, young tree." My eyes were misting. "Stand strong. Yours is a valued treasure."

He was awake when I got home. I leaned over his bed. "I checked on the tree," I told him. "It's growing."

He smiled.

The Life Jacket

August 9, 1942, had already been a bad day for Elgin Staples—and it was only getting worse! In truth, all his troubles had begun the day before. As a Signalman 3rd Class in the U.S. Navy during World War II, he'd been stationed on the USS *Astoria* battleship and sent to patrol the Pacific Ocean in search of Japanese warships.

On August 8, 1942, in what would be known as the Battle of Savo Island, the *Astoria* engaged the Japanese flagship *Chokai* in a heated conflict. Sirens wailed and men yelled instructions as Signalman Staples took his position on the deck. As the day wore into night, Elgin and his fellow soldiers scored one direct hit on the *Chokai*, then a second. Cheers went up among the Americans —but were all too quickly silenced when the American cruiser suffered crippling damage from the Japanese attack.

Around two o'clock in the morning on August 9, disaster struck for Elgin Staples. He was standing near the number one gun turret on the *Astoria* when it suddenly exploded! Shrapnel flew in all directions, wounding the young signalman in both legs and sweeping him off the ship into the roiling sea. Dazed and in a state of semi-shock, the young soldier barely remembered the life belt he was wearing, then with one swift motion he activated the simple trigger mechanism that enabled the belt to keep him afloat and prevent him from drowning.

For the next four hours, Staples floated in and out of consciousness, bobbing up and down in the ocean water while the fiery battle raged around him. Finally, at six A.M., Elgin was rescued by a passing destroyer and returned to his ship, the USS *Astoria*. That was when his bad day started getting worse.

Badly damaged in the firefight, the *Astoria* was actually sinking! In desperation, the cruiser's captain tried to run his ship aground in hope of saving her—but the attempt failed. Within hours of his rescue, Signalman Elgin Staples found himself back in the ocean watching his powerful battleship sink to the depths below. Once again, his life belt was faithful, keeping the still-wounded soldier afloat until he could be rescued once more around noon on August 9, 1942. This time he—along with five hundred other survivors—was placed on the USS *President Jackson* where he received medical attention and was evacuated away from the battle zone.

It was while he was on the *President Jackson* that Elgin finally regained enough of his senses to realize his life had been saved not once, but twice by that life belt around his waist. Curious, he took a closer look at the life belt and discovered it had been manufactured at the Firestone Tire and Rubber Company of Akron, Ohio. He also found a registration number on the belt. Grateful for the excellent service of that little piece of equipment, he quickly memorized the registration number so he could ask his mother—a Firestone employee—exactly what it meant.

Soon after, Elgin was sent back to the States to recover from his injuries. While there he told his mother about his life belt and mentioned it had a registration number on it as well. His mother explained that Firestone insisted every employee take personal responsibility for the war effort, and because of that, each product inspector was given a unique identification number. That person's number was then affixed to every product that inspector approved so that if any defective product was discovered it could be traced back to the individual responsible for allowing it to leave the company.

Curious, Elgin quoted the number he'd found on his own life belt, the one that had twice rescued him from certain death. After a shocked moment of silence his mother replied:

"Elgin, that's my number."

ON THE EXCELLENCE OF PRAYER

Author Unknown

Prayer is like:
- A pitcher—to carry the water of life.
- A chemist—that turns all of life into gold.
- Incense—with which to worship God.
- A bow—to carry the arrow of our need.
- The porter—to watch the door of our lips.
- The guard—to keep the fort of our heart.
- The hilt of a sword—to defend our hands.
- A master workman—who accomplishes things.
- A barometer—to show our spiritual condition.
- The chariot—to hold our petitions, the Spirit being its wheels.
- The key to life—to wind us up in the first place, and keep it going each day thereafter.

THE RICHES OF SIMPLICITY*

by Phil Callaway

We live in a small town, population 3417 (including pets). No traffic lights. No malls. No frills. You sneeze while driving past and you'll miss us every time. We've had opportunity to live elsewhere, but this is the suit that fits us best for now.

Some of my best friends are city folk. They love the bustle. The noises. The choices. They thrive on cell phones. On lunch meetings. On car-pool lanes.

Not me. Many weekends you'll find me in the city, but when I point my car toward home it's like someone loosened my tie. I enjoy living on a street that's so quiet you can sit on your back porch and listen to the sun set. I enjoy getting up each day knowing that a ten-minute walk to work will clear my sinuses, and that if I left my car lights on the night before, a neighbor probably went out in his slippers and shut them off.

In a recent cover story, "Why Americans Are Fleeing to Small Towns," *Time* magazine pointed out that in the 1990s two million more Americans moved from cities to rural areas than migrated the other way. Jim Wiley of Wilmington, Ohio, was one. In the article he says, "Living in Los Angeles, my vision became blurred and twisted. I was spoiled. I had secretaries doing everything for me. All I did was talk on the phone and sit in traffic. In L.A. I endured fifteen solid years of sunshine. All those rays every day—they aggravated me."

Living in a small town can blur your vision, too. You see, it's easier here to slow down to an unhealthy crawl. To sit on the porch each evening watching the bug-zapper and forgetting that there's a world out there that could use my help. That's when I need to remember that slowing down in a speeded-up world does not mean taking a permanent exit to Easy Street. God does not call us to rest seven days a week with our head in the sand. He calls us to make an impact wherever we are. But in order to do that, it's important to slow down and focus on the things that matter most. Remember His words, "Be still, and know that I am God" (Psalm 46:10 NIV), and ". . .in quietness and trust is your strength" (Isaiah 30:15 NIV).

The other day I asked my eleven-year-old son Stephen, "If you had your life to live over again, what would you do differently?" Before he knew I was kidding, he answered, "Eat more candy."

I laughed at first, but the more I thought about his words, the more I realized the wisdom in them.

You see, I have yet to hear someone in an old folks' home say, "I wish I would have spent more time with my computer," or, "I wish I would have worried more and laughed less." But I know too many who are spending the last half of a busy life regretting the first half.

A frenzied friend of mine has this on his desk: "We the willing, led by the unknowing, are doing the impossible for the ungrateful. We have done so much for so long with so little we are now qualified to do anything with nothing."

Late in life, an anonymous friar in Nebraska monastery wrote the following words. I sent them to my friend. He's still trying to get up enough nerve to show them to his boss.

If I had my life to live over again, I'd try to make more mistakes next time.

I would relax, I would limber up, I would be sillier than I have been on this trip.

I know of very few things I would take seriously.

I would take more trips. I would be crazier.

I would climb more mountains, swim more rivers, and watch more sunsets.

I would do more walking and looking.

I would eat more ice cream and less beans.

I would have more actual troubles, and fewer imaginary ones.

You see, I'm one of those people who lives life prophylactically and sensibly hour after hour, day after day. Oh, I've had my moments, and if I had to do it over again, I'd have more of them.

In fact, I'd try to have nothing else, just moments, one after another, instead of living so many years ahead each day. I've been one of those people who never goes anywhere without a thermometer, a hot-water bottle, a gargle, a raincoat, aspirin, and a parachute.

If I had it to do all over again, I would go places, do things, and travel lighter than I have.

If I had my life to live over, I would start barefooted earlier in the spring and stay that way later in the fall.

I would play hookey more.

I wouldn't make such good grades, except by accident.

I would ride on more merry-go-rounds.

I'd pick more daisies.

Of course, I'm not for playing hookey (believe me, my kids know this), but sometimes I wonder where I got the notion that God is only pleased with my work. In the same way that I love to watch my children chase one another down a sandy beach, so God is pleased when we go barefoot. In the same way that I cheer when my daughter sinks a basketball (yes, this has happened), so God is pleased when we play.

When I was a boy, I heard people say that it's better to burn out than to rust out, and I found myself wondering if there wasn't a better alternative. Years later I've noticed that some of those very same people are the most miserable humans I know. In chasing dreams they missed waking up to the simple joys around them. In climbing a ladder they have failed to see that it was leaning against a crumbling wall.

I haven't arrived yet. I'm still learning to juggle a busy schedule while enjoying the simple gifts God gives. I'm still learning that there is freedom in slowing down. That there are riches in simplicity. And most of all, I'm learning that there is freedom in following the example of Jesus. After all, He carried the weight of the world on His shoulders, but slept soundly in the bottom of a storm-tossed boat. After all, He changed the course of history and still had time to hold little children on His lap.

Will you determine with me to forget keeping up with the Joneses? To stop chasing things we can't cram in our coffins?

Whether you find yourself in the car-pool lane or out watching the bug-zapper, it can make all the difference.

⁂

When Life Gives You Hayfeet. . .*

by Mike Nappa and Dick Olson

"These farm boys are hopeless! They'll never be soldiers! Why can't somebody send us real men to train for this war?"

That was the growl of many army officers from both the North and the South during America's Civil War. Trouble was, they were most often right! That's because when the Civil War began, rural farm boys streamed into the military from all over the country, anxious to fight for their side in the war. At first, the Union and Confederate armies welcomed these young men, but soon it became apparent that the "backward" ways of these uneducated country boys could be more of a hindrance than a help in the war effort. These troops had a long way to go before they could be called an excellent fighting machine—and many a woebegone general was certain they'd never go far with such poor fighting stock.

The officers' biggest frustration came when it was time to teach these raw recruits to march. Many of the rural boys had never learned to distinguish their left sides from their right sides. Because of this, the standard marching cadence, "Left, left, left, right, left!" simply caused chaotic confusion among the ranks.

Still, while all the other officers grumbled, one creative man decided to make soldiers out of these country folk. He decided to quit complaining and instead work to bring out the best in what he'd been given. Knowing that farm boys had learned the difference between hay and straw, he made his recruits tie hay to their left feet and straw to their right. Then he revised his cadence to "Hayfoot, hayfoot, hayfoot, strawfoot, hayfoot." Other officers picked up the practice, and in short time, these young country boys were marching machines, uniformly stomping their hayfeet in and out of battle with the best of them.

While other officers wasted time complaining

about the polished recruits they didn't have, one creative officer chose to invest his time in learning how to achieve excellence out of the tools he already had. We'd be wise to do the same.

SPEAKING OF EXCELLENCE. . .

"Make good or make tracks."
Cowboy proverb,
as recorded by KEN ALSTAD
in *Savvy Sayin's*

"Genius is one percent inspiration and ninety-nine percent perspiration."
THOMAS ALVA EDISON,
as quoted by Robert Burleigh in
Who Said That?

"If at first you do succeed, try not to look astonished."
from a bumper sticker

*"Winning is a habit.
Unfortunately, so is losing."*
VINCE LOMBARDI,
as quoted by GEORGE HETZEL, JR., in
The Coaches' Little Playbook

"I won't have any money to leave behind. I won't have the fine and luxurious things of life to leave behind. But I just want to leave a committed life behind."

REV. MARTIN LUTHER KING, JR.,
as quoted by Jim Haskins in
*I Have a Dream: The Life and
Words of Martin Luther King, Jr.*

"People of mediocre ability sometimes achieve outstanding success because they don't know when to quit. Most men succeed because they are determined to."

ALFRED A. MONTAPERT, in
Words of Wisdom to Live By

*"You have achieved excellence
as a leader when
people will follow you anywhere,
if only out of curiosity."*
GENERAL COLIN L. POWELL,
as quoted by LORNE A. ADRAIN in
The Most Important Thing I Know

*"You must do the thing
you think you cannot do."*
ELEANOR ROOSEVELT,
as quoted by ROBERT BURLEIGH in
Who Said That?

"No one is compelled to serve great causes unless he feels fit for it, but nothing is more certain than you cannot take the lead in great causes as a half-timer."

WINSTON CHURCHILL,
as quoted by FREDERICK TALBOTT in
Churchill on Courage

*"We are what we repeatedly do.
Excellence, then, is not an act,
but a habit."*
ARISTOTLE, as recorded on
Quoteland.com

❧

THE WORD ON EXCELLENCE. . .

But indeed I also count all things loss for the excellence of the knowledge of Christ Jesus my Lord, for whom I have suffered the loss of all things, and count them as rubbish, that I may gain Christ.   PHILIPPIANS 3:8 NKJV

But as it is written: "Eye has not seen, nor ear heard, nor have entered into the heart of man the things which God has prepared for those who love Him."   1 CORINTHIANS 2:9 NKJV

*In all the work you are doing,
work the best you can.
Work as if you were doing it for the Lord,
not for people.
Remember that you will receive
your reward from the Lord,
which he promised to his people.
You are serving the Lord Christ.*
COLOSSIANS 3:23–24 NCV

Choose my instruction instead of silver, knowledge rather than choice gold, for wisdom is more precious than rubies, and nothing you desire can compare with her.   PROVERBS 8:10–11 NIV

Therefore, my dear brothers, stand firm. Let nothing move you. Always give yourselves fully to the work of the Lord, because you know that your labor in the Lord is not in vain.

1 CORINTHIANS 15:58 NIV

With his trademark wit, author Tim Wildmon has shared a fresh perspective on the need for excellence in life. Listen—and laugh—as he shares his wisdom with you here.

CHICKEN*

by Tim Wildmon

"Whatever you do, do it all for the glory of God," is what the Bible says (1 Corinthians 10:31 NIV). Even at work? Yes, I'm convinced even at work, no matter what your vocation may be.

One of the interests I have in meeting new people is to ask them what they do for a living. It takes all kinds to make this ol' world go around. I am most intrigued when I meet someone with an occupation that I know I could never do, no matter how much training I had.

Take air traffic controllers, for instance. Never. I'm the kind of guy who absolutely has to get up and go get some coffee several times during the workday. I just don't think I would work out in the tower.

"Yeah there, flight 407 or 704 or whatever your number is, just sit tight 'cause I got to run down the hall and get a cup of coffee. Might have to brew. Now, if you don't mind, why don't you just slow down a little—just a li'l—over Iowa so I don't lose you on my screen. In fact, I'm gonna put a yellow sticky right here where you are now and I'll catch up with you in a few minutes. Talk among yourselves."

I'd be afraid I'd get something in my eye at an inopportune moment, or that I might mistake a fly on the screen for a plane. And have you ever tried to understand a commercial pilot? These are very smart and talented people, but let's be honest, most sound half awake when they welcome you aboard—which is not a comforting feeling when you're already seated.

"Um, thank you, ladies. . .flying. . .bumps. . . errr. . .any 'sistence. . .err. . .O'Hare 'round. . . err. . .relax. . ."

Passengers who actually care what the pilot says—mostly first-time flyers—look around at each other, shaking their heads, trying to put slurred or mumbled words together into understandable sentences. They don't want to be the one to disobey an order from the cockpit and cause the plane to crash. So they want to know what was growled lowly over the loudspeaker.

Every once in a while you get a pilot who can actually articulate and speak clearly in complete sentences. But more often than not, pilots on loudspeakers are like doctors writing prescriptions; you can't make heads or tails of it. I don't know which is more dangerous, a pilot who can't speak or a doctor who can't write.

Or how about mechanical engineers? Are you kidding me? In the first place I couldn't pass algebra, even if I were still taking it, and secondly, my mechanical skills end at the on-off button. And I can pump gas. But if it's not working at my house, don't look at me to fix it. My wife Alison told me to quit faking it a long time ago and I gladly obliged. I couldn't go on living a lie.

Once, when we were still newlyweds, she asked me about something having to do with our car's engine. The car was making a weird sound. Not wanting to let her know so soon in our happily-ever-after that I knew absolutely nothing about an automobile's engine—or engines in general, for that matter—I answered her, "Well, baby, it kind of sounds like the medulla oblongata to me."

"What?" Alison asked from the bedroom.

"Yeah, it's shaped real oblong with a gata jutting out the side. I'll see if I can't get one down at Auto Zone and put it in myself tomorrow," I bluffed. She called my bluff.

This next job I read about just about beats all I've ever heard. The story was out of a magazine called *AOPA Pilot*—obviously a publication for pilots. It read, and as Dave Barry would say, I'm not making this up:

"Learjet and an independent manufacturer of Learjet cockpit windshields are having a shootout, so to speak.

"When Perkins Aircraft of Fort Worth, Texas, offered the windshields at $10,000 less than the Learjet parts price last year, Learjet fired back with a service information letter warning customers that the windshields were not chicken tested. That is, the FAA did not require Perkins to prove that the windshields could survive a bird impact at approximately 300 knots (350 mph).

"To simulate the bird strike, Learjet tests its windows using a cannon that fires a chicken at 300 knots toward a stationary cockpit."

Now, think about this for a minute, ladies and gentlemen. Picture this if you will. No, really, go ahead and imagine this workstation.

I have a lot of questions here that beg to be asked.

In the first place, who builds these cannons that fire off the fowl? Cannons R Us? I mean, there can't be a great demand for these machines, can there? Did the folks at Learjet pick this baby up at a trade show of some kind after watching the demo? Are there chicken-launcher repairmen out there who go to school—like copier repairmen—to learn their trade and show up at the office every few days?

"How do, Bill?"

"Oh, pretty good. Yourself?"

"Not bad. Say, you think we need a new chicken launcher? This is the third time I've seen you out here this week. When's the warranty run out anyway?"

"Well, I've ordered a part from Angola, and once it comes in I think we can get you a few more miles out of that 1993 model. Although, I gotta tell you, and I'd get fired for saying this, but just between us boys, they just don't make chicken launchers like they used to, Tom. Why, in the mid-eighties me and the Maytag repairman, we were tight. Always golfing and fishing. Not anymore. Not since they started making these machines overseas."

Secondly, what qualifications do you need to operate a chicken launcher? Did Learjet interview twenty people before finally finding their man? Is there some institution of higher learning that gives a degree in chicken launching? Or did they just take Ed out of the mailroom?

"Ed, we're moving you today to our new wing, so to speak. Your new position will be more of a challenge for you, Ed. We're confident you'll do just fine. Besides, this new job will be in one area so you won't have to be always running around like a chi. . . Well, you'll see what I mean."

And what does Ed tell folks when asked what he does for a living? What do his kids tell the other kids at school when asked what their daddy does for a living? Do schools take field trips to watch chicken launching?

Does Ed pull up his goggles, wipe his brow, and

look down at his watch at about 11:30 anticipating lunch break? What does he think about as he loads one chicken after another? What does his machine sound like when it's clicking on all cylinders? I wonder, *How do you know if you've had a good day or a bad day at work? Do you get stressed out? Do you ever go to KFC for lunch?* Like I said, I've got a million questions.

The Bible says in Proverbs 16:3 that we are to commit our work to the Lord. Whatever it is that we do in life (including our vocation), as long as it's honest and moral, can be used by God to bring glory to Himself. I don't care what it is.

An honest day's work is a powerful witness to a boss who perhaps doesn't know the Lord. The boss and one's coworkers notice you going the extra mile without complaint. I know; I am a boss. Whatever it is that you do, do it as unto the Lord and that includes a good attitude. Even if it's chicken launching. Although, after an extensive check by the author, the Bible doesn't seem to address this particular vocation specifically.

Well, I don't have any answers to the perplexing questions I posed a couple paragraphs back. However, I think it's safe to say that this department will not be featured on any television advertisement, à la General Motors or Ford, showing Ed at work with the voice of James Earl "This is CNN" Jones saying: "Meet Learjet's Ed

Walters, making your safety his first priority."

≈

If you've read any of our previous books, then you know we rate few things as more excellent than that wondrous, silky-sweet substance, chocolate! In fact, our deeply theological view is that chocolate is evidence of God. . .but that's another story.

Meanwhile, we feel honored to include Mary Carter's excellent article on this excellent substance for you in this (we hope) excellent book. So sit back, grab a bon bon (or two), and read on to enjoy. . .

A NEARLY COMPLETE GUIDE TO CHOCOLATE*

by Mary K. Carter

There are two very different types of people. Type A is bewitched by chocolate. Type B is content with a bag of potato chips. When a Type A is in the mood for chocolate, which is often, nothing else will do. Type A's have a deep and personal relationship with the stuff. We talk to it. It talks to us. Chocolate says, "I'm in the cabinet—come and find me." When we search for it our pulses quicken and our brows glisten with sweat. We look forward to the day after Valentine's Day, when we get chocolate hearts for half price. The average American eats over nine pounds of chocolate per year. Actually, I think the Type B's leave it alone so the Type A's can each have eighteen pounds. That's only about six ounces per week— just half a bag of chocolate chips, for goodness' sake. It only seems fair for the B's to bow out.

A Brief History of Chocolate

The word chocolate comes from the Aztec Indian word *xocolatl*, meaning "bitter water." These Indians made a drink by pounding theobroma cocoa beans into a powder, then mixing it with spices. Theobroma means "food for the gods," as the Aztecs believed the bean was sent from the heavens. Theobroma cocoa is what we still call the bean today. The Aztec Indians served their unsweetened drink hot, like coffee or tea. The Spanish found it too bitter and are believed to be the first chocolate lovers who added sugar. This opened a new door for sweets lovers. The sugared hot drink became popular all over Europe.

Chocolate wasn't popular in America until nearly two hundred years later. It was first manufactured in Massachusetts, in 1765, when it became available as a national product. Even then, however, it wasn't widely used. In fact, cocoa powder, as we know it, wasn't produced here until

1828. Thomas Jefferson preferred hot chocolate to tea or coffee. Like many others at that time, he believed it to be a restorative.

Now for the names we've all heard of. By 1842, the Cadbury Company of England had developed a process of combining sugar, chocolate, cocoa butter, and dairy products that resulted in chocolate made in bar form. The Swiss chocolatier, Henri Nestle, followed by adding sweetened condensed milk—the first milk chocolate. Milton Snavely Hershey, of Lancaster, Pennsylvania, manufactured the first American-made milk chocolate bar in 1894. To say the least, it became even more popular. Something that was almost unheard of in America only twenty years before became a daily treat for many.

How is it made?

This amazing theobroma cocoa bean is somewhat like a green bean because it grows in a pod. They're picked by hand and placed in perforated boxes where they ferment in the open air. Cocoa trees grow twenty degrees on either side of the equator, thriving only in a hot and rainy climate. Each tree is good for just twenty to thirty pods per year. Each pod only has about twenty-five to forty beans—and it takes four hundred beans to make a pound of chocolate. After harvesting, the beans are dried, sacked, and shipped to chocolate plants. The shells are removed after the beans have been roasted in a machine called a "cracker and fanner." This separates the nibs and the shells and blows away the debris. The cocoa shells are popular these days in gardening because they make a most fragrant mulch. So, maybe it wasn't your imagination when you thought your neighbor's yard smelled good enough to eat.

Cocoa beans are about 50 percent fat, called "cocoa butter," and 50 percent liquid, called "chocolate liquor." The cocoa butter is expressed as a gold liquid. The chocolate liquor becomes a thick paste. Cocoa powder is made by melting the chocolate liquor to press out even more of the cocoa butter. This mass is ground into powder. This is what is used to make baking or cooking chocolate.

Sweet chocolate for candy is a mixture of chocolate liquor, sugar, and vanilla. These are blended together until very smooth, and combined with cocoa butter. Milk chocolate is the result of this same process, only there's more sugar, more cocoa butter, and some milk. It's processed further to remove excess moisture and to make it smooth. Semi-sweet chocolate has less sugar.

A Guide to the Different Types of Chocolate
Any Type A can tell you that the beauty of each kind of chocolate is in the mouth of the beholder. Some prefer a nearly black and velvety Swiss dark chocolate. Yet another chocolate

lover might find happiness in any creamy milk chocolate bar made. Here are some of the most popular types of chocolate, and their most common uses in cooking.

- Cocoa powder. Unsweetened, dried, and pulverized chocolate liquor. Most of the cocoa butter has been processed out, leaving a dry and dark powder that's ideal for cooking. It's such a simple form that a cook can work with it in unlimited ways. Just as a painter faces an empty canvas, with his palette of colors in hand, the Type A cook stands before the many ingredients imagining the chocolate possibilities.
- Semisweet and bittersweet. This chocolate liquor has cocoa butter, vanilla, and a scant amount of sugar added. The amount of sugar determines the name. Bittersweet has less than semisweet. Unsweetened, of course, has no sugar at all.
- Milk chocolate. This most popular chocolate is a blend of chocolate liquor, cocoa butter, milk solids, sugar, and vanilla. It's better for eating than for baking.
- White chocolate. Actually, this is not chocolate at all because it contains no chocolate liquor. It is made of cocoa butter, milk solids, sugar, and flavorings. Look for those with cocoa butter rather

than vegetable oil. Its quality is superior. Almond bark is a vegetable oil product. It has its uses, but it doesn't claim to be a chocolate product, and you will find that the almond bark melts more slowly and leaves a film in your mouth. It's waxy.

- Coating chocolate. This chocolate is used in candy making, mostly by professionals. It has such a high cocoa butter content that it's difficult to work with because it melts so quickly.

So, there you have it. An almost complete guide to chocolate. And if you're a Type A, like me, you probably hear chocolate calling your name by now. You better go find it.

A Chocolate Primer

- Chocolate, unless it's ice cream or mousse, should be served at room temperature. When it is cold, the waxy texture interferes with the flavor.
- Ideal storage temperature for chocolate is seventy-eight degrees. When it is slightly melted, and then becomes solid again, it has a chalky gray cast called a bloom. It is harmless. This only means that the fat content has risen to the surface of the bar. It doesn't hurt the flavor.

- When a recipe calls for a one-ounce square of unsweetened chocolate, and you only have cocoa powder in your pantry, you can safely substitute by using three tablespoons of cocoa powder and one tablespoon of butter in your recipe.
- If your recipe calls for grated chocolate, *do* refrigerate the bar until it is cold enough to handle. Work quickly with the end wrapped in waxed paper so you can grate it without it melting.
- When you intend to melt the chocolate, there are several successful methods. The key is to always remember to keep the heat source low. And don't be in a hurry. A double boiler is probably the safest way to ensure that the chocolate melts evenly and does not burn. The quickest method, the microwave, is also the trickiest. Use a low setting and check the texture of the bar or chips every fifteen seconds. When the chocolate begins to lose its shape, and becomes shiny, it is done. Remove it from the oven and set it aside. The heat inside the chocolate will spread and melt the rest. Stir it to be certain the melting is even.
- Four cups of cocoa equals one pound.
- One square of chocolate (one ounce) results in four tablespoons when grated.
- One ounce of unsweet chocolate and four

teaspoons of sugar can be substituted for 1⅔ ounces semi-sweet.

- Read all labels carefully. Semi-sweet, bitter-sweet, unsweet, milk chocolate, dark chocolate, etcetera, can be confusing. Be sure you're buying the product you want.

PRAYER FOR AN EXCELLENT LIFE

by Saint Patrick

Christ, be with me, Christ before me,
    Christ behind me,
Christ in me, Christ beneath me,
    Christ above me,
Christ on my right, Christ on my left,
Christ where I lie, Christ where I sit,
    Christ where I arise,
Christ in the heart of everyone who
    thinks of me,
Christ in every eye that sees me,
Christ in every ear that hears me.
    Salvation is of the Lord,
    Salvation is of the Christ,
    May Your salvation, O Lord,
      be ever with us.

Prayer for an Excellent Life
Part 2

by Amy Nappa

Christ, be with me. . .and please bring a little chocolate, too! AMEN!

❧

In case you were wondering, God has planned for us the most excellent home in all of eternity, so we think it appropriate to end this chapter with the Bible's description of that place. And while we're thinking of it, let's plan on meeting each other there someday. We hear the chocolate will be out of this world. . .

A Most Excellent Reward
Revelation 21:1–22:6 NIV

Then I saw a new heaven and a new earth, for the first heaven and the first earth had passed away, and there was no longer any sea. I saw the Holy City, the new Jerusalem, coming down out of heaven from God, prepared as a bride beautifully dressed for her husband. And I heard a loud voice from the throne saying, "Now the dwelling of God is with men, and he will live with them. They will be his people, and God himself will be with them and be their God. He will wipe every tear from their eyes. There will be no more death or mourning or crying or pain, for the old order of things has passed away."

He who was seated on the throne said, "I am making everything new!" Then he said, "Write this down, for these words are trustworthy and true."

He said to me: "It is done. I am the Alpha and the Omega, the Beginning and the End. To him who is thirsty I will give to drink without cost from the spring of the water of life. He who overcomes will inherit all this, and I will be his God and he will be my son. But the cowardly, the unbelieving, the vile, the murderers, the sexually immoral, those who practice magic arts, the idolaters and all liars—their place will be in the fiery lake of burning sulfur. This is the second death."

One of the seven angels who had the seven bowls full of the seven last plagues came and said to me, "Come, I will show you the bride, the wife of the Lamb." And he carried me away in the Spirit to a mountain great and high, and showed me the Holy City, Jerusalem, coming down out of heaven from God. It shone with the glory of God, and its brilliance was like that of a very precious jewel, like a jasper, clear as crystal. It had a great, high wall with twelve gates, and with twelve angels at the gates. On the gates were written the names of the twelve tribes of Israel. There were three gates on the east, three on the north, three on the south and three on the west. The wall of the city had twelve foundations, and on them were the names of the twelve apostles of the Lamb.

The angel who talked with me had a measuring rod of gold to measure the city, its gates and its walls. The city was laid out like a square, as long as it was wide. He measured the city with the rod and found it to be 12,000 stadia in length, and as wide and high as it is long. He measured its wall and it was 144 cubits thick, by man's measurement, which the angel was using. The wall was made of jasper, and the city of pure gold, as pure as glass. The foundations of the city walls were decorated with every kind of precious stone. The first foundation was jasper, the second sapphire, the third chalcedony, the fourth emerald, the fifth sardonyx, the sixth carnelian, the seventh chrysolite, the eighth beryl, the ninth topaz, the tenth chrysoprase, the eleventh jacinth, and the twelfth amethyst. The twelve gates were twelve pearls, each gate made of a single pearl. The great street of the city was of pure gold, like transparent glass.

I did not see a temple in the city, because the Lord God Almighty and the Lamb are its temple. The city does not need the sun or the moon to shine on it, for the glory of God gives it light, and the Lamb is its lamp. The nations will walk by its light, and the kings of the earth will bring their splendor into it. On no day will its gates ever be shut, for there will be no night there. The glory and honor of the nations will be brought into it. Nothing impure will ever enter it, nor will anyone who does what is shameful or deceitful, but only those whose names are written in the Lamb's book of life.

Then the angel showed me the river of the water of life, as clear as crystal, flowing from the throne of God and of the Lamb down the middle of the great street of the city. On each side of the river stood the tree of life, bearing twelve crops of fruit, yielding its fruit every month. And the leaves of the tree are for the healing of the nations. No longer will there be any curse. The throne of God and of the Lamb will be in the city, and his servants will serve him. They will see his face, and his name will be on their foreheads. There will be no more night. They will not need the light of a lamp or the light of the sun, for the Lord God will give them light. And they will reign for ever and ever.

The angel said to me, "These words are trustworthy and true. The Lord, the God of the spirits of the prophets, sent his angel to show his servants the things that must soon take place."

8

Anything

*P*raiseworthy

PRAISEWORTHY: (adjective) (1) worthy of
praise; (2) laudable. Synonyms: estimable,
deserving, praisable, thankworthy, glorious,
exalted.

THE PICTURE

The picture still haunts me, though really there's nothing all that frightening about it. I've seen worse on the evening news, or in the daily newspaper. Yet still, it's Maurits Escher's painting that flashes in my mind during still moments—just before sleep; gazing out the window; traveling silently down endless miles of freeway.

I can see it in my mind, and it fills me with wonder and sadness.

It's not a fancy painting, really. Simply a woodcut work of art, made by carving a stamp on the surface of a block of wood, dipping the design in ink, then stamping the inked wood on a page. The result is a blocky, black-and-white image. Hardly something to compare to Michaelangelo.

But bringing his considerable talent to bear, in 1928 Escher created a woodcut that captures a moment in history that no one has really seen. With exquisite detail and mathematical precision, Escher has framed the Tower of Babel for me in a way I'll never forget.

Open your mind's eye with me a moment, and let's take a look at this unusual masterpiece. The first thing you'll notice is the perspective. Escher has given us a God's-eye view, looking down at an angle on the impressive structure these men have made. The ground is eons away, it seems. Towering like a colossus over minute shaded buildings and blocking even an expanse of the sea, this is truly a man-made marvel.

Look a little more closely, and now you can see supplies scattered all around the ground. Piles of lumber, ropes and pulleys that climb all the way to the top. Shirtless muscled workers dot the scene, from ground to ledges to window, to the apex of the tower. At first glance, it appears this place is a bustling center of activity. Things are being done here—great things. That much is obvious.

And yet, something is wrong. For all its progress, the building itself seems silent. Look closely at the workers. Some are fighting, others gazing down from ledges with their hands in the air. A few are simply sitting down, for a rest perhaps? Some are even stretched out in mock slumber.

Look again at the pulleys. All ropes seem usable, and the pulley system has the power to connect workers from the top of the building to the ground thousands of feet below.

But all pulleys lead to nowhere. All activity accomplishes nothing. The mighty man-made undertaking has abruptly, and permanently, ceased.

Classical art expert Keith J. White comments on this moment frozen into the woodcut images on Escher's canvas, saying, "Technically, it all seems feasible (there is still adequate rope and material) but it has grown too big. The limits of human endeavor have been reached."

We are seeing this tower just moments after God has stepped into the picture. With barely a thought, He has confused the language of the workers, bringing this grand tower to a grinding halt. What was once a mighty testament to the power and will of man has now become a mockery of the same.

The tower stands unfinished, in disarray, broken and useless. In time thieves will strip it of valuables. Rain, wind, and sun will weaken and erode the mighty structure. It will crumble to dust, leaving nothing but a memory.

God, on the other hand, will remain. Powerful, majestic, eternal. Nothing humanity can create will ever compare to God. Period.

And so I find myself awed and silent when I gaze at this picture. For, you see, I have my own towers, and I'll bet you have them, too. They may not be as conspicuous as the mighty Tower of Babel, but they're there. You know it and I know it.

Careers, social standing, homes, success, families, children, power, respect, salaries, and more. All are little towers in their own ways. Yet, unless God is involved, all our efforts to build these monuments to our lives will, like the Tower of Babel, cease. They, too, will crumble into eternity, leaving less than dust behind.

The simple truth is no matter what I do, no matter how praiseworthy my goals, my efforts will always be man-made efforts. In the end, they, too, will wilt and die if they must stand alone.

Which brings me back to the picture. If you look closely at the top of the tower, seated on a corner of half-finished brick and mortar is a worker. His face is toward heaven, his arms are outstretched. He, of all people, seems to have seen the Almighty God when He came to visit.

As I look closely at that worker, I realize he knows what I am just now learning: The only object truly worthy of our praise is God Himself. Nothing more; nothing less.

And that makes all the difference in life.

❧

PSALM 150 (NIV): A HYMN OF PRAISE

Praise the LORD.
    Praise God in his sanctuary;
    praise him in his mighty heavens.
    Praise him for his acts of power;
    praise him for his surpassing greatness.
    Praise him with the sounding of the
        trumpet,
    praise him with the harp and lyre,

praise him with tambourine and dancing,
praise him with the strings and flute,
praise him with the clash of cymbals,
praise him with resounding cymbals.
Let everything that has breath praise the
    LORD.
Praise the LORD.

MOTHER TERESA ON
LIVING A PRAISEWORTHY LIFE

Let us all become a true and fruitful branch on
the vine Jesus, by accepting Him in our lives as
it pleases Him to come:

as the Truth to be told;
as the Life to be lived;
as the Light to be lighted;
as the Love to be loved;
as the Way to be walked;
as the Joy to be given;
as the Peace to be spread;
as the Sacrifice to be offered;
in our families and our neighbors.

Sometimes we are slow to give praise where it is due. Perhaps we can learn a lesson from the one Jess Moody calls. . .

THE MAN WHO CHANGED THE WORLD*

by Jess Moody

The historians missed it. The encyclopedias have it down wrongly. A Russian inventor, Vladimir Zworykin, is officially given the credit. Yet the scientific community is beginning to awaken to a fact that might revise their evaluation of it.

What is it?

Television.

Zworykin gets the credit for inventing it.

Philo P. Farnsworth did it; but he may never receive that designation because he had a problem that caused him never to receive the plaudits for his astonishing accomplishment.

The apostle Paul said something about it. Prejudice may have stood in the way—because of Farnsworth's "problem."

Farnsworth worked on a farm, plowing a straight line on a potato farm; yet his mind was far away, thinking through the electronic puzzle as to how to transmit moving pictures through the air. Here he was, a person with no electronic training and no engineering background. Also, he was completely out of step with the entire scientific world as to how to go about seeking a solution to the large enigma.

Coupled with his problem, no one was giving him even a moment's notice to be seriously considered as a contender in this frenetic chase to find the answer to photographic transmission without the aid of wires to interconnect between sending and receiving the visual transmission.

The scientists in London, Moscow, and New York had been struggling to find the solution to this dilemma, and they were aided by large grants that enabled them to pursue every avenue of research to solve it. So, what chance did this Farnsworth have, a potato farmer with no education in the sciences, and with his problem plaguing his every step?

While plowing, he imagined a different approach. He imagined dividing a screen into long rows. Just like the field he was plowing, using electricity to create areas of light and darkness at each point along the row. Then stacking the rows on top of each other, he imagined that they could bring to focus a picture.

Bingo! The results were better than anything the world of science had ever conceived. It is the very system used today.

Farnsworth struggled all his life to receive credit for his marvelous invention—but he never received historical credit, mainly because of his problem. What makes this story even more incredible is that Farnsworth was born in a log cabin. One can see the makings of a whole chapter in the future history books, but Farnsworth's problem denied him his limelight.

He had a propensity toward science, a completely logical left brain, a vivid imagination from his right brain, coupled with a photographic memory. His mind could analyze automobile malfunctions, electric battery chargers, and just about any mechanical concept imaginable. Yet, he would only now be recognized because people have come to see that his problem was not a hindrance. The problem lay in the prejudice of others regarding his problem, not in the problem itself.

When he was eleven years old, the Farnsworth family moved to Idaho's Snake River. This delighted him because there they had electricity, which was the main seed fertilizing his mind to seek "wonder after wonder and every wonder true," as Saint Brude said.

In the attic of the old house, he discovered reams of old scientific magazines and journals. He spent endless hours devouring those publications, feeding his "dream machine."

The years came and went, and young Farnsworth tinkered with ideas that made his peers think of him as somehow "wacky on science," the oddball in his society.

As he read of the scientific search concerning sending moving pictures through the air, instinctively he knew they were on the wrong track. He became enthralled with his study of the electron. Science was seeking some moving parts as a key to picture transmission. Philo Farnsworth knew better—but no one would listen, mainly because of his problem.

The girl who later became his wife hesitated to marry him because he would become ecstatic talking about moving pictures flying through the air, space travel, and assorted electronic wonders.

An inspiring teacher, Justin Tolman, patiently listened as the boy wrote his theories of light-picture movement through the air. He almost covered the chalkboard with his theories. Later, after the discovery, Farnsworth reminisced that it was Tolman's encouragement that fired up his determination to continue, in spite of his interfering problem.

Two businessmen, George Everson and Les Gorrell, took special interest in Farnsworth's ideas. They each invested their entire life savings in Philo's research. They overlooked his problem, showed faith in him, putting a total of twelve thousand dollars into his inventive genius, a lot of money in those days. Farnsworth moved to Los Angeles and feverishly worked day and night, quickly using up the investors' money; but they never lost faith in him and borrowed twenty-five thousand dollars to control the feverish race against the other inventors of the world.

He perfected the instrument, filed for a patent, which was refused until they could prove that it worked. So, on September 7, 1927, Farnsworth transmitted history's first electronic television picture by sending the picture of a glass slide with a straight line in it from one room to another. Farnsworth had done it!

David Sarnoff, then president of Radio Corporation of America, sent the Russian scientist Vladimir Zworykin to visit Farnsworth, who naïvely told everything about the invention. Sarnoff took the invention, heralded the Russian as the inventor, and spent huge sums of money announcing it to the world.

Farnsworth never received credit for his invention until many years later, 1957, on the game show *I've Got a Secret.* He was paid eighty dollars for appearing.

It was there that Philo Farnsworth revealed to an audience of forty million people not only his invention, but also his problem. He summed it all up in one sentence. "I invented electronic television when I was fourteen years old." His problem was his extreme youth.

The apostle Paul recognized the same problem when he said, "Let no man despise thy youth" (1 Timothy 4:12 KJV).

Later, as an old man, Philo sat with his wife, Pam, and watched as man made "one small step for man; one giant leap for mankind." Man had set foot on the moon, just as Philo, a bright boy, had told her when he was courting her. And it was on worldwide television.

"You know, Pam," he said, "it makes it almost worthwhile."

❧

SPEAKING OF PRAISE. . .

"The sweetest of all sounds is praise."
XENOPHON, as recorded on
Quoteland.com

"Christ is the Alpha and Omega, the beginning and the end of everything. All times and ages belong to Him. To Him be glory forevermore. May the light of Christ, the light of faith, continue to shine. . . . May no darkness ever extinguish it!"
POPE JOHN PAUL II,
in *Fear Not*

"The measure of a life,
after all, is not its duration,
but its donation."
CORRIE TEN BOOM,
as quoted by JOHN MAXWELL in
It's Just a Thought

"Always remember you're unique—just like everyone else."   from a bumper sticker

"God is mightiest in power, fairest in beauty, immortal in existence, supreme in virtue; therefore, being invisible to every mortal nature, He is seen through His works themselves."

ARISTOTLE
in *De Mundo*

*"Our God is an awesome God;
He reigns from heaven above!"*
RICH MULLINS, in the song
"Awesome God"

"I don't claim anything of the work. It is His work. I am like a little pencil in His hand. That is all. He does the thinking. He does the writing. The pencil has nothing to do with it. The pencil has only to be allowed to be used."

MOTHER TERESA, in a 1986 speech
to the Awakening Conference

"Wish I could crash like the waves or turn like the autumn leaves in an effort to praise You!"

WATERMARK, in the song "Gloria"
from their self-titled album

"We should give God the same place in our hearts that He holds in the universe."

ANONYMOUS

"Oh, gaze of love, so melt my pride that I may
in Your house but kneel and in my brokenness to
cry, spring worship unto Thee"

JARS OF CLAY,
in the song "Hymn" on
their *Much Afraid* album

❧

THE WORD ON PRAISE. . .

*Let another praise you,
and not your own mouth;
someone else, and not your own lips.*
PROVERBS 27:2 NIV

The words of the wise bring them praise, but the
words of a fool will destroy them.

ECCLESIASTES 10:12 NCV

*Great is the LORD!
He is most worthy of praise!
His greatness is beyond discovery!*
PSALM 145:3 NLT

I call upon the LORD, who is worthy to be
praised, and I am saved from my enemies.

PSALM 18:3 NASB

"Then I looked, and I heard the voice of many angels around the throne, the living creatures, and the elders; and the number of them was ten thousand times ten thousand, and thousands of thousands, saying with a loud voice: 'Worthy is the Lamb [Jesus] who was slain to receive power and riches and wisdom, and strength and honor and glory and blessing!' "

REVELATION 5:11–12 NKJV

※

CAT SCRATCH FEVER

The young woman felt her heart skip a beat. Could it be? She dared not hope too hard. Yet she couldn't resist the temptation to kneel and begin a silent prayer.

She had seen the goddess before, but never this close. She'd caught glimpses of her at the temple in her home city, Bubastis, Egypt. The young wife had gone there to pray and do her religious duties. Temples like that one dotted the skyline in many cities in her home country, and were filled with ornate statues and magical inscriptions of tribute to the great goddess.

The young woman held her breath despite herself. All was silent. Had Bastet-the-goddess so quickly left this poor mortal? She renewed her prayer with earnestness, offering praise to the deity of good fortune and good health. Then, to hedge her bets a bit, she also offered scraps of praise to the sun god, Ra. After all, didn't he battle each night with Apep, the serpent of darkness, and emerge victorious again each morning? And didn't he receive help from his good and faithful daughter, Bastet, even taking on her form for his fight?

She closed her eyes and prayed ever more fervently, worshiping the image she had seen only moments ago. She now clutched a worn amulet of Bastet and her children, and in her prayer reminded Bastet that she, too, wanted children—as many children as were carved into this precious amulet, in fact!

The young woman opened her eyes and a smile froze on her face. There, sitting right in the doorway of her own house, the goddess Bastet had appeared! She bowed low before the image, offering a continuous stream of praise and worship.

And in the doorway the alleycat paused, licked its forepaws, stretched and yowled, then casually lost interest and went on its way in search of its next meal. And through it all, the little tabby was blissfully unaware that it had just been the object of worship for a poor, deceived woman of ancient Egypt.

The young believer watched the cat stroll away, confident she had just seen God. Little did she know that she'd wasted her devotion on a common, household cat.

Which makes one wonder, *If people from days of old could be tricked into worshiping something as silly as a cat, what are we being tricked into worshiping today? Jobs perhaps? Money? A lover? Status, prestige, influence, power, education, non-education, philosophies, rugged independence, the earth itself, aliens from space, and more?*

Perhaps we'd be wise to remember that only Jesus Christ deserves to be worshiped. Time spent in devotion to anything else is only wasted time—worth no more than a prayer directed to a cat.

❧

Not long ago Mike was granted an interview with gospel music legend Andrae Crouch. During that time, Andrae shared a bit about praising God. Listen as Mike describes what Pastor Crouch had to say. . .

ANDRAE CROUCH
ON THE POWER OF PRAISE

The music of Andrae Crouch has long been cause for celebration throughout the halls of the churches of the world. Few artists have accomplished more than he has over the last two or three decades. Consider (deep breath!):

Crouch has recorded fifteen albums—and sold millions of them, won nine Grammy Awards, collaborated with artists from Elvis Presley to Michael Jackson to Whitney Houston to Michael W. Smith, worked on musical scores for movies such as *The Lion King, Free Willy,* and *The Color Purple,* been nominated for an Academy Award, performed for presidents and kings, and contributed dozens of songs to your church's hymnal.

Not bad for a guy with no formal music training, who can't sight-read music, who had to overcome stuttering as a boy, and who continues to struggle with dyslexia. Still, Crouch maintains that the lyrics he wrote twenty-five years ago are as true today as they were back then: "Through it all; Through it all; I've learned to trust in Jesus; I've learned to trust in God."

The words of "Through It All" were especially meaningful when first Crouch's mother, then his father, then his brother all died within a span of two years. "Probably the hardest time in my life," sighs Pastor Crouch. "Just getting through the gloom, the grieving part of it and to learn the reason why.

"Many of the songs I've written speak to me as far as telling me the process of how to get through things. 'Through It All,' in particular, lets me know you have a lot of experiences in life and you [must] learn to trust Jesus."

Still, with his family members passing so quickly, Andrae readily admits he had difficulty at times trusting Jesus, feeling angry at God instead. It all came to a head one day during prayer. Like David writing a psalm, Crouch says he laid his soul bare before God, being very honest about his feelings of grief and loss.

"I thought I was just going to crack up," relates Crouch. "I said, 'Lord, You took my mother!' I just told Him like that and I said, 'After all this, You took her so suddenly and it really grieved my heart.' I told Him I thought that was cold-blooded."

Crouch says, "I knew I'd never, ever forget my mother. I'd never smell her perfume. Never hear her voice. Never taste her cooking and never feel her warm body against mine. And it just got too big. It was unbearable. The tears would not stop because that was my mother. I loved her."

In the midst of that prayer, Crouch felt strongly that God was encouraging him to praise God. He could almost hear God's voice saying, "You've written a lot of songs I've given you about praise and worshiping Me in things, not for things, but in things."

Like a petulant child, Crouch admits he refused at first, praying, *I cannot praise You going through this. I cannot do it. I don't feel like it.* But after struggling inwardly for a half-hour or so, he finally gave in.

"I just started saying, 'Thank You, Jesus,' and 'I praise You, Jesus.' And then I felt strength come like a gushing well. The joy of the Lord came in the room and filled my soul. And probably for four hours I was praising God and jumping and praising God."

Through that experience Crouch says he learned a valuable lesson, "If depression comes for anything, learn to praise Him. I know I've written a whole bunch of songs about that, but I learned it myself. It's incredible—the power of praise."

❦

AN AFRICAN CANTICLE

All you big things, bless the Lord,
Mount Kilimanjaro and Lake Victoria,
The Rift Valley and the Serengeti Plain,
Fat baobabs and shady mango trees,
All eucalyptus and tamarind trees,
Bless the Lord.
Praise and extol Him for ever and ever.

All you tiny things, bless the Lord,
Busy black ants and hopping fleas,
Wriggling tadpoles and mosquito larvae,
Flying locusts and water drops,
Pollen dust and tsetse flies,

Millet seeds and dried dagaa,
Bless the Lord.
Praise and extol Him for ever and ever.

❧

Worship*

*by Mike Nappa, Amy Nappa,
and Michael Warden*

"All people have a need to worship," says Christian musician Ron Stinnett. "And nowhere is this need more obvious than at a rock concert."

According to Stinnett, people at a rock concert exhibit the same characteristics and actions as people at worship. "Look around the audience during a concert," he says. "Kids are raising their hands in the air, swaying to the music, clapping, singing, shouting for joy; some are moved to tears, some are moved to laughter, and all are somehow moved. It's a pseudo worship experience for everyone involved."

Watching people at a rock concert can reveal to us humankind's deep-seated need to worship. The same might be said about watching people at a sporting event, people at a parade, or men and women gathered at a political rally. As Stinnett puts it, "When people have a passion and an interest and love for something, they naturally exhibit attitudes and actions of worship toward it. What God desires is that [we] have a passion, interest, and love for Jesus. The natural result will be worship of God."

Although teenagers may unknowingly "worship" outside the church, few of them are experiencing worship within the church walls. According to a Search Institute study, Christian teenagers rate "meaningful worship" as the fourth-highest influence on their faith development, but less than half (47 percent) say their church provides this. Yet two-thirds (66 percent) still say they have a "responsibility to worship God."

Even Christian adults struggle with actually worshiping in church. About four out of ten say they "rarely" or "never" experience God's presence during a worship service. As pollster George Barna says, "Calling a church service 'a time of worship' does not always make it so."

Intimate worship of God also seems absent from the personal lives of many Christians. According to recent surveys by the Barna Research Group, about one out of three Christians reports never feeling as if he or she is in God's presence. Another 13 percent say they've felt as if they were in God's presence only once or twice in their lives.

When we give God our worship, He draws us closer to Himself (see James 4:8). But like their adult counterparts, many [young] people have not yet experienced the intimate power inherent in worshiping God. Until they do, they'll have to settle for the "pseudo worship" of rock concerts and sporting events.

What people need to know about worship:
We can learn to experience true worship by understanding these core truths: that worship involves reverence of, praise and adoration for, and service to God; that worship can be a personal experience; and that worship can be a group (or corporate) experience.

Worship involves reverence of, praise and adoration for, and service to God. The Hebrew word translated worship literally means "to bow down to." It refers to showing honor and reverence to a superior being. God is the only One Who is truly worthy of this worship. Christian educator Lawrence Richards points out that "in Revelation, worship clearly has the sense of praise and adoration." And Romans 12:1 reminds us that a life of sacrificial service to God is "the spiritual way for you to worship."

Because worship is all of these things, we can have great freedom—the freedom to worship God each day of our lives. Our worship doesn't have to be confined to a church's walls. It can happen anywhere, any time we have an attitude of reverence, praise, and service to God.

We can be loud in worship, be quiet in worship, move around in worship, sit still in worship, meditate on God in worship, serve God's people in worship—the possibilities are endless! And when we learn to worship God in commonplace situations and everyday ways, we can more readily experience the presence of God in our lives.

Worship can be a personal experience. Personal worship involves times of verbally or silently expressing praise and gratitude to God. But personal worship is also a lifestyle of caring about and helping people who are hurting. (See 2 Samuel 22:4; Psalms 28:7, 34:1; Micah 6:8; John 4:19–24; and Romans 12:1.)

It's during times of personal worship that we can recognize God's power at work in our individual lives—and give God thanks and praise for His interest and actions in our lives. During these intimate times with God, we experience what it means to be in the presence of our loving, caring Father. As gospel music legend Andrae Crouch described it in his song "Quiet Times" (from his album *This Is Another Day*), "That's when I tell You [God] that I love You, and You remind me that You love me, too."

Worship can be a group (or corporate) experience. Lawrence Richards says, "Although worship is a matter of heart and an expression of one's inner relationship with God, it may also be a public expression of a corporate relationship with God."

Scripture seems to validate this view. Mark 14:26 mentions (almost in passing—as if we should have known they'd do this anyway) that Jesus and disciples sang a hymn in corporate worship. Acts 8:27 tells us about an Ethiopian who traveled a great distance to worship with others in Jerusalem. Psalm 95:6–7 is a call for people to gather and worship God together. Luke 19:37–38 records the story of a time when a crowd of people shouted joyful praise to Jesus. And Acts 2:46–47 reveals that the people of the early church often spent time together in worship.

What a great example we have! We, like the early church, can gather regularly for the excitement of a group time of worshiping God.

And according to Ron Stinnett, "That beats a rock concert or sporting event any day!"

❧

As D. James Kennedy and Jerry Newcombe eloquently reiterate in the following essay, truly none is more praiseworthy than Jesus Christ Himself!

CHRIST AND CIVILIZATION: QUICK OVERVIEW OF CHRIST'S IMPACT ON WORLD HISTORY*

by D. James Kennedy and Jerry Newcombe

Some people have made transformational changes

in one department of human learning or in one aspect of human life, and their names are forever enshrined in the annals of human history. But Jesus Christ, the greatest man who ever lived, has changed virtually every aspect of human life—and most people don't know it. The greatest tragedy of the Christmas holiday each year is not so much its commercialization (gross as that is), but its trivialization. How tragic it is that people have forgotten Him to whom they owe so very much.

Jesus says in Revelation 21:5, "Behold, I make all things new." (Behold! [*idou* in Greek]: "Note well," "look closely," "examine carefully.") Everything that Jesus Christ touched, He utterly transformed. He touched time when He was born into this world; He had a birthday and that birthday utterly altered the way we measure time.

Someone has said He has turned aside the river of ages out of its course and lifted centuries off their hinges. Now, the whole world counts time as Before Christ (B.C.) and A.D. Unfortunately, in most cases, our illiterate generation today doesn't even know that A.D. means Anno Domini, "In the year of the Lord."

It's ironic that the most vitriolic atheist writing a propagandistic letter to a friend must acknowledge Christ when he dates that letter. The atheistic Soviet Union was forced in its constitution to acknowledge that it came into existence in

1917, in the "year of our Lord." When you see row after row of books at the library, every one of them—even if it contains anti-Christian diatribes—has a reference to Jesus Christ because of the date.

The Growth of the Mustard Seed

Jesus said that the kingdom of heaven is like a mustard seed, which is tiny in and of itself; but, when fully grown, it provides shade and a resting place for many birds. This parable certainly applies to an individual who embraces Christ; it also applies to Christianity in the world.

Christianity's roots were small and humble—an itinerant rabbi preached and did miracles for three and a half years around the countryside of subjugated Israel. And today there are more than 1.8 billion professing believers in Him found in most nations on earth! There are tens of millions of today who make it their life's aim to serve Him alone.

Emperors and governors were the men with power in Christ's day. But now their bodies rot in their sepulchres, and their souls await the Final Judgement. They have no followers today. No one worships them. No one serves them or awaits their bidding.

Not so with Jesus! Napoleon, who was well accustomed to political power, said that it would be amazing if a Roman emperor could rule from the grave, and yet that is what Jesus has been doing. (We would disagree with him, though, in that Jesus is not dead; He's alive.) Napoleon said: "I search in vain in history to find the similar to Jesus Christ, or anything which can approach the gospel. . .nations pass away, thrones crumble, but the Church remains."

A Quick Overview

Despite its humble origins, the Church has made more changes on earth for the good than any other movement or force in history. To get an overview of some of the positive contributions Christianity has made through the centuries, here are a few highlights:

- Hospitals, which essentially began during the Middle Ages.
- Universities, which also began during the Middle Ages. In addition, most of the world's greatest universities were started by Christians for Christian purposes.
- Literacy and education for the masses.
- Capitalism and free-enterprise.
- Representative government, particularly as it has been seen in the American experiment.
- The separation of political powers.
- Civil liberties.
- The abolition of slavery, both in antiquity and in more modern times.

- Modern science.
- The discovery of the New World by Columbus.
- The elevation of women.
- Benevolence and charity; the good Samaritan ethic.
- Higher standards of justice.
- The elevation of common man.
- The condemnation of adultery, homosexuality, and other sexual perversions. This has helped to preserve the human race, and it has spared many from heartache.
- High regard of human life.
- The civilizing of many barbarian and primitive cultures.
- The codifying and setting to writing of many of the world's languages.
- Greater development of art and music. The inspiration for the greatest works of art.
- The countless changed lives transformed from liabilities into assets to society because of the gospel.
- The eternal salvation of countless souls!

The last one mentioned, the salvation of the souls, is the primary goal of the spread of Christianity. All the other benefits listed are basically just by-products of what Christianity has often brought when applied to daily living. . .

When Jesus Christ took upon Himself the

form of man, He imbued mankind with a dignity and inherent value that had never been dreamed of before. Whatever Jesus touched or whatever He did transformed that aspect of human life. Many people will read about the innumerable small incidents in the life [of] Christ while never dreaming that those casually mentioned "little" things were to transform the history of humankind.

If Jesus Had Never Been Born

Many are familiar with the 1946 film classic *It's a Wonderful Life,* wherein the character played by Jimmy Stewart gets a chance to see what life would be like had he never been born. In many ways this terrific movie directed by Frank Capra is the springboard for this book. The main point of the film is that each person's life has impact on everybody else's life. Had they never been born, there would be gaping holes left by their absence. My point [here] is that Jesus Christ has had enormous impact—more than anybody else—on history. Had He never come, the hole would be a canyon about the size of a continent.

Christ's influence on the world is immeasurable. . . .

But Some People Wish Christ Had Never Been Born

Not all have been happy about Jesus Christ's

coming into the world. Friederich Nietzsche, the nineteenth-century atheist philosopher who coined the phrase "God is dead," likened Christianity to poison that has infected the whole world. He said of Jesus: "He died too early; He Himself would have revoked His doctrine had He reached" greater maturity!

Nietzsche said that history is the battle between Rome (the pagans) and Israel (the Jews and the Christians); and he bemoaned the fact that Israel (through Christianity) was winning and that the cross "has by now triumphed over all other, nobler virtues." In his book *The Anti-Christ,* Nietzsche wrote:

"I condemn Christianity; I bring against the Christian Church the most terrible of all the accusations that an accuser has ever had in his mouth. It is, to me, the greatest of all imaginable corruptions; it seeks to work the ultimate corruption, the worst possible corruption. The Christian Church has left nothing untouched by its depravity; it has turned every value into worthlessness, and every truth into a lie, and every integrity into baseness of soul."

Nietzsche held up as heroes a "herd of blond beasts of prey, a race of conquerors and masters." According to Nietzsche, and later Hitler, by whom or what were these Teutonic warriors corrupted? Answer: Christianity. "This splendid ruling stock was corrupted, first by the Catholic laudation of feminine virtues, secondly by the Puritans' plebeian ideals of the Reformation, and thirdly by inter-marriage with inferior stock." Had Jesus never come, wailed Nietzsche, we would never have had the corruption of "slave morals" into the human race. Many of the ideas of Nietzsche were put into practice by his philosophical disciple, Hitler, and about sixteen million died as a result.

In *Mein Kampf,* Hitler blamed the Church for perpetuating the ideas and laws of the Jews. Hitler wanted to completely uproot Christianity once he had finished uprooting the Jews. In a private conversation "shortly after the National Socialists' rise to power," recorded by Herman Rauschning, Hitler said:

"Historically speaking, the Christian religion is nothing but a Jewish sect. . . . After the destruction of Judaism, the extinction of Christian slave morals must follow logically. . . . I shall know the moment when to confront, for the sake of the German people and the world, their Asiatic slave morals with our picture of the free man, the god-like man. . . . It is not merely a question of Christianity and Judaism. We are fighting against the perversion of our soundest instincts. Ah, the God of the deserts, that crazed, stupid, vengeful Asiatic despot with his powers to make laws! . . . That poison with which both Jews and Christians have spoiled and soiled the free, wonderful instincts of man and lowered them to the level of doglike fright."

Both Nietzsche and Hitler wished that Christ had never been born. Others share this sentiment. For example, Charles Lam Markmann, who wrote a favorable book on the history of the ACLU, entitled *The Nobles Cry*, said: "If the otherwise admirably civilized pagans of Greece and their Roman successors had had the wit to laugh Juda-ism into desuetude, the world would have been spared the two thousand year sickness of Christendom."

Interestingly, people living under Nazi oppression, under Stalin's terror, under Mao's cultural revolution, and the reign of the Khmer Rouge were all spared "the two thousand year sickness of Christendom"! . . . Contrary to Markmann's armchair philosophizing, civil liberties have been bequeathed by Christianity and not by atheism or humanism.

Stalin and Mao both tried to destroy Christianity in their respective domains. In the process, they slaughtered tens of millions of professing Christians, but they utterly failed in their ultimate objective.

In one sense, the point [is] to say to Nietzsche, Freud, Hitler, Robert Ingersoll, Lenin, Stalin, Mao, Madalyn Murray O'Hare, Phil Donahue, the ACLU, and other leading anti-Christians of the past and present, that the overwhelming impact of Christ's life on Planet Earth has been positive, not negative. . . .

From transforming the value of human life to transforming individual lives, the positive impact of Jesus Christ is felt around the globe.

❧

In the end, Christ is all that matters. For that reason we're happy to end this chapter—and this book—with these words of testimony and praise for. . .

ONE SOLITARY LIFE

Author Unknown

He was born in an obscure village, the child of a peasant woman. He grew up in another village, where He worked in a carpenter shop until He was thirty. Then for three years He was an itinerant preacher. He never wrote a book. He never held an office. He never had a family or owned a home. He didn't go to college. He never visited a big city. He never traveled two hundred miles from the place where He was born. He did none of the things that usually accompany greatness. He had no credentials but Himself.

He was thirty-three when the tide of public

opinion turned against Him. His friends ran away. One of them denied Him. He was turned over to His enemies and went through the mockery of a trial. He was nailed to a cross between two thieves.

While He was dying, His executioners gambled for His garments, the only property He had on earth. When He was dead, He was laid in a borrowed grave through the pity of a friend. Nineteen centuries have come and gone, and today He is the central figure of the human race.

All the armies that ever marched, all the navies that ever sailed, all the parliaments that ever sat, all the kings that ever reigned, put together, have not affected the life of man on this earth as much as that one solitary life.

CREDITS

ABOUT THE AUTHORS

Mike and Amy Nappa are founders of the Christian media organization Nappaland Communications, Inc. and creators of the webzine for families at www.Nappaland.com. They are also the best-selling authors of *A Heart Like His* (Barbour) and other books, and have over a half-million copies of their books in print. Additionally, Mike and Amy both serve as contributing editors for *CBA Frontline* magazine; are Internet columnists for several web sites including Crosswalk.com, iBelieve.com, CBNnow.org, and others; and write monthly columns for *HomeLife* and *FaithWorks* magazines. Their writing has appeared in many fine publications such as *CCM*, *Children's Ministry*, *Christian Parenting Today*, *Christian Single*, *ParentLife*, *FamilyFun*, *Focus on the Family Clubhouse*, *Clubhouse Jr.*, *Group*, *Living with Teenagers*, *New Man*, *Profile*, *Release*, and more. The Nappas make their home in Colorado where they're active in their church. To contact Mike and Amy, access their webzine at: www.Nappaland.com.

Inspirational Library

Beautiful purse/pocket-size editions of Christian classics bound in flexible leatherette. These books make thoughtful gifts for everyone on your list, including yourself!

A Heart Like His   A challenging, encouraging, and fun look at the godly characteristics described in Ephesians 5:22–23—the Fruit of the Spirit.
Flexible Leatherette $4.97

When I'm on My Knees   The highly popular collection of devotional thoughts on prayer, especially for women.
Flexible Leatherette $4.97

The Bible Promise Book   Over 1,000 promises from God's Word arranged by topic. What does God promise about matters like: Anger, Illness, Jealousy, Love, Money, Old Age, and Mercy? Find out in this book!
Flexible Leatherette $3.97

Daily Wisdom for Women   A daily devotional for women seeking biblical wisdom to apply to their lives. Scripture taken from the New American Standard Version of the Bible.
Flexible Leatherette $4.97

Available wherever books are sold.
Or order from:

Barbour Publishing, Inc.
P.O. Box 719
Uhrichsville, OH 44683
http://www.barbourbooks.com

If you order by mail add $2.00 to your order for shipping.
Prices subject to change without notice.